CW00418933

Fr. Augustus Tolton

Deacon Harold Burke-Sivers

➤• Fr. Augustus •◆
TOLTON

The Slave Who Became
the First African-American Priest

EWTN PUBLISHING, INC.
Irondale, Alabama

EWTN Publishing, Inc.
5817 Old Leeds Road, Irondale, AL 35210

Distributed by Sophia Institute Press, Box 5284, Manchester, NH 03108.

Library of Congress Cataloging-in-Publication Data

Names: Burke-Sivers, Harold, author.
Title: Fr. Augustus Tolton : the slave who became the first African-American
  priest / Deacon Harold Burke-Sivers.
Description: Irondale, Alabama : EWTN Publishing, Inc., 2018. Includes
  bibliographical references.
Identifiers: LCCN 2018031389 ISBN 9781682780589 (pbk. : alk. paper)
Subjects: LCSH: Tolton, Augustine, 1854-1897. Catholic Church — United
  States — Clergy — Biography. African American clergy — Biography.
Classification: LCC BX4705.T6813 B87 2018 DDC 282.092 [B] — dc23 LC record
available at https://lccn.loc.gov/2018031389

First printing

For Colleen, Claire, Angela, Benjamin, and Sophia

Contents

Fr. Augustus Tolton

Introduction

Sister Caroline Hemesath's powerful narrative of Fr. Augustus Tolton's life, *From Slave to Priest: A Biography of the Reverend Augustine Tolton,*[1] is a poignant reminder that with God all things are possible. Sister Hemesath acquaints us with the first black American priest and chronicles the profound struggle for equality and acceptance black Catholics faced in the period after the Civil War. Confronted with a succession of seemingly insurmountable challenges — escaping from slavery, his father's death, abject poverty, exclusion from American seminaries — Fr. Tolton's fervent desire to study Catholicism, his intense longing for the priesthood, and his mother's loving support were the wellsprings from which he drew the strength to persevere.

Fr. Tolton knew that unconditional trust in God meant that he must become completely vulnerable before his Creator. He reveled in the folly of divine abandonment, confidently exposing the

---

[1] Caroline Hemesath, S.S.F., *From Slave to Priest: A Biography of the Reverend Augustine Tolton (1854–1897), First Black American Priest of the United States* (San Francisco: Ignatius Press, 2006). Fr. Tolton was baptized under the name Augustus. Many sources through time have standardized this to Augustine, but his cause for canonization uses his given name, so we will use that throughout.

deepest parts of his soul before God, who gave him the strength to exercise his priestly ministry under the weighty yolk of racism. He was a beacon of hope to black Catholics in the nineteenth century who were trying to find a home in the American Church. Fr. Tolton, in his abiding faith and selfless charity, was the instrument through which God's love shone brightly. The resplendent refrain "I have come ... not to do my own will, but the will of him who sent me" echoed majestically throughout his brief life (John 6:38).

Despite the hardships placed on Fr. Tolton by a culture firmly rooted in the arid soil of racial hatred, God brought him out of the heart of darkness and used him as an instrument of grace. He was a tireless messenger of the gospel who "was not afraid to go into the Deep South, where racial hatreds had reached a high pitch and where segregation was decreed by harsh laws."[2] Despite the novelty of being the only black priest in an otherwise all-white clergy, the gifted Fr. Tolton was able to convey effectively the richness, beauty, and truth of the Catholic Faith, which penetrated even the hardest hearts. His biographer attests: "Wherever he went, he was respected and honored."[3]

When we look beneath the surface of our national life, we see that the septic undercurrent of racism flows largely unabated. Racism is intricately woven into the fabric of American culture. But unlike the 1950s and 1960s, when racism was overt, extreme, and statutorily institutionalized, the structure of racism today is subtler and more covert, exhibiting itself in recurrent outward manifestations of what has become an unconscious and tacit philosophy of dehumanization.

Since the civil rights era, black Catholics, in response to racism in the Church, have often turned to and been heavily influenced

[2] Ibid., 170.
[3] Ibid.

by liberation theology, a Christian belief in the transcendent as a vehicle for social liberation. Liberation theology does not ask what the Church is, but rather what it means to be the Church in the context of liberating the poor and the oppressed. As such, in liberation theology the Church's primary mission is to challenge oppression and identify Herself with the poor. On this view, the Magisterium (that is, the teaching authority of the Church) is allied with the oppressive class by definition, since it does not participate in the class struggle. Ultimately, in this version of Catholicism, faith is subordinate to political ideology, and the Church becomes an instrumental good rather than an intrinsic good as the necessary means of salvation.

Fr. Tolton, a former slave who became a Catholic priest, knew well that the basis for any authentic theology of liberation must be the truth about Jesus, the Church, and the dignity of man. He endured years of frustration, humiliation, and rejection in a country that boasts of its commitment to religious freedom and toleration. Despite the fact that slaves were "free," they were far from liberated. In Fr. Tolton's own words: "We are only a class—a class of dehumanized, brutalized, depersonalized beings."[4] The nation failed the test of "freedom" rooted in its own Declaration of Independence, while the Catholic Church in America failed to live up to Her own creed and gospel, not recognizing that genuine liberation means freedom from the bondage of both iniquity and sin.

With the assistance and support of several persistent and undaunted priests, Fr. Tolton was finally accepted by the Catholic Church—in Rome! He thrived in the Eternal City, where his priestly vocation was nurtured and where his gifts and talents were recognized, prompting even the prefect of the Sacra Congregatio

---

[4] Ibid., 101.

de Propaganda Fide[5] to note what the American Church failed to appreciate: "Fr. Tolton is a good priest, reliable, worthy, and capable. You will discover that he is deeply spiritual and dedicated."[6] For his part, Fr. Tolton acknowledged the great gift of his Catholic Faith and, despite bitter trials, remained faithful to the teachings of the Church. He was a visionary who saw beyond race and politics, looking inward—into the heart of the Church Herself. He taught, "The Catholic Church deplores a double slavery—that of the mind and that of the body. She endeavors to free us of both.... She is the Church for our people."[7]

The life of Fr. Tolton is a study in faithful obedience. When the Vatican assigned Fr. Tolton to serve as a missionary priest in the United States, where he was "a slave, an outcast, a hated black,"[8] he obeyed in faith. His was not the faith of blind obedience, like that of an automaton. Rather, as a child of our Heavenly Father, in humility and generosity he strove to discern and fulfill the will of God under the loving guidance and direction of the Holy Spirit. It is precisely *in altum*—into the deep, the void, the unknown—that Fr. Tolton followed his mission to be a fisher of men (see Luke 5:1–11).

The greatest legacy of Fr. Augustus Tolton is not simply that he was a pioneer, the first black American priest in the United States. Yes, he was that—but he was so much more! Fr. Tolton loved and served the Lord with great fervor and intensity. He knew that God's love is so immense, its power so limitless, its embrace so tender

---

[5] In English, the Sacred Congregation for the Propagation of the Faith, which was responsible for missionary work. Today, this part of the Curia is known as the Congregation for the Evangelization of Peoples.

[6] Hemesath, *Slave to Priest*, 151.

[7] Ibid., 171.

[8] Ibid., 145.

and intimate that Love Himself brings forth life. Fr. Tolton was a living testimony to God's creative, life-giving work.

Fr. Tolton serves as a role model for those who seek to be configured more perfectly to Christ. Amidst great persecution, he showed us that being configured to Christ means emptying ourselves so that God can fill us; it means exposing the weakest parts of who we are so that God can make us strong; it means becoming blind to the ways of this world so that Christ can lead us; it means dying to ourselves so that we can rise with Christ.

I pray that everyone who reads this book will be inspired by Fr. Augustus Tolton, who, guided by the Holy Spirit, became a living example of what it means to be fully alive in our Catholic Faith.

Chapter 1

Fr. Augustus Tolton: A Short Biography

The Early Years

Augustus John Tolton, the second of three children, was born into slavery on April 1, 1854, in Brush Creek, Missouri. His baptismal record reads, in part, "A colored child.... Property of Stephen Eliot."[9] His mother, Martha Jane Chisley, was given as a wedding gift to the Eliot family, on whose plantation she met and married Augustus's father, Peter Paul Tolton. When Augustus was seven years old, his father died in the Civil War, fighting for the belief that all men, including blacks, are equal and should have the same rights and privileges as whites.

That same year, the remaining members of the Tolton family escaped from slavery via the Underground Railroad to Quincy, Illinois. Shortly after their arrival, Augustus and his siblings were enrolled at St. Boniface Catholic School, where they were taunted with harsh, racialized insults by classmates. Many parents threatened to remove their children and withhold financial support from the parish. The pressure from the white parents and parishioners

---

[9] Hemesath, *Slave to Priest*, 28. It was a common practice for slaves, whether they arrived from Africa or were born in the United States, to be baptized into the religion of their Christian owners. This was the case with the Tolton family.

soon became too great for the family to bear. Mrs. Tolton withdrew the children from school.

Augustus found work in a tobacco factory and helped support his family. After work, a small group of dedicated nuns and priests taught him to read and write in both English and German, which fostered his love for learning. (He later learned Latin and French as well.) One of these priests was Fr. Peter McGirr, pastor of the nearby St. Peter's parish and school. He admired Augustus and recognized his abilities and was convinced that Augustus should receive a Catholic education, and so he invited him to attend St. Peter's school. Aware of Augustus's experience at his previous school, Fr. McGirr "prepared himself for any unpleasantness or trouble that might arise" and "redoubled his resolution not to be intimidated or dissuaded by the parishioners."[10] When Fr. McGirr welcomed the Toltons with open arms, the reaction was swift and vicious: Some parishioners threatened the pastor with violence; others petitioned the bishop, asking for Fr. McGirr's removal; and some even vowed to leave the Catholic Faith entirely if the Tolton family remained in the parish.[11] With the help of the School Sisters of Notre Dame, who promised to teach Augustus when others refused, Fr. McGirr defied the parishioners and admitted Augustus, who attended school during the winter months, when the tobacco factory was closed.

---

[10] Ibid., 49.

[11] This attitude was prevalent in many communities throughout the northern United States where blacks had made their way to freedom and began establishing themselves. In 1866, the United States Catholic bishops met at the Second Plenary Council in Baltimore and demanded that all possible means be implemented for the religious care and instruction of blacks. Due to threats of hostility and violence, however, the majority of white Catholics, who wanted blacks to establish their own churches, largely ignored the directives of this local synod.

Augustus became an altar server and quickly memorized the Latin prayers for Mass. At the age of sixteen, he received his first Holy Communion, and, during Fr. McGirr's homily, in which he explained the meaning of the Holy Eucharist and the Sacrifice of the Mass, Augustus's heart, in his own words, "leapt with a strange exhilaration."[12] It was on that day that young Augustus envisioned himself becoming a priest.

Realizing the depth of Augustus's "genuine faith and integrity,"[13] Fr. McGirr became convinced that the boy was meant for the priesthood, and he encouraged and nurtured his fledgling vocation. Augustus received the sacrament of Confirmation at age eighteen and graduated "with distinction" from St. Peter's. It was the summer of 1872.

The Struggle for Acceptance

Soon after commencement, Fr. McGirr, with the aid of another priest, helped Augustus to apply to the Franciscan Order — where he was met with the first of many rejections. Undaunted, Fr. Mc-Girr secured the promise of the diocesan bishop to fund Augustus's seminary training if a seminary could be found that would take him. Fr. McGirr wrote to every seminary in the United States, and all of them rejected a Negro candidate.

There was some hope, however, that at least one religious community would be open to a black seminarian. The St. Joseph Society for Foreign Missions (today known as the Josephites) established a mission at the Church of St. Francis Xavier in Baltimore expressly to evangelize freed blacks. In 1875, another priest who supported Augustus's cause, Fr. Theodore Wegmann, contacted the Josephites

---

[12] Hemesath, *Slave to Priest*, 53.
[13] Ibid., 55.

about him. They informed Fr. Wegmann that they had no seminary in the United States and suggested that Augustus become a catechist; then, if accepted by their order in London, he could become a missionary priest in Borneo.

While enthused by the prospect of becoming a missionary priest, Augustus was beset by a series of setbacks, most notably the reassignment of several priests who were overseeing his academic and spiritual formation. This forced the Tolton family to relocate to Missouri, where the brilliant yet troubled and unstable Fr. Patrick Dolan took over Augustus's studies. An alcoholic, Fr. Dolan neglected Augustus's studies and informed him that, in his parish, only white boys were allowed to be acolytes at Mass.

Augustus took a job in a saloon, where he experienced firsthand the degradation of humanity among the men and women who "sacrificed their dignity to wallow [in] the stench of reeking bodies, alcoholic fumes and stale tobacco [that] pervaded the entire atmosphere."[14] Not making any progress toward the priesthood in Missouri, the Toltons moved back to Quincy.

Augustus was more determined than ever to be a priest. He found a job making horse collars, and Fr. Francis Reinhart, chaplain at St. Mary's Hospital and assistant pastor at St. Boniface Church, took over his studies. Augustus next took a job in a soda factory for twelve dollars a week, which allowed him more time for study. Fr. Reinhart was reassigned in 1878, and, with the help of yet another sympathetic, supportive priest, Augustus registered at St. Francis Solanus College (now Quincy University), where he studied mathematics, science, and literature.

Encouraged and assisted by Franciscan Fr. Michael Richardt and Sister Herlinde Sick, Augustus began teaching Sunday school to Negro children. Sister Hemesath relates the results:

[14] Ibid., 80.

The silent, unobtrusive activity of Augustine Tolton was largely responsible for the apostolate to the blacks of Quincy. Both he and his mother were tireless in their efforts to reinstate members of their race in the Church and to encourage others to study the Catholic religion.... Augustine understood the problems and temptations of his race; he knew the underlying causes of weakness and degradation in which many were steeped. With all his heart he deplored the lack of spiritual guidance and opportunities for rehabilitation open to untutored and downtrodden blacks. Yet, he could understand why some white people were hostile, why many Catholics were indifferent, and why those in positions of authority in the Church sometimes vacillated.[15]

Priesthood at Last!

In 1879, at the age of twenty-five, Augustus learned that the local bishop's attempt to have him admitted to the seminary in Rome had been unsuccessful. At the time, the Vatican accepted candidates for the priesthood from countries without seminaries in order to prepare them for a life of missionary work. But Rome was naïvely optimistic about the Catholic Church in the United States, believing that Augustus could and should be trained in America, where the freed slaves needed priests. The Vatican did not fully appreciate that, although America had many seminaries for a nation still considered mission territory, the Church in America had consistently failed to live up to the tenets of Her own creed and gospel. The bishop recommended that Augustus wait a few more years until the Josephites could open a seminary in Baltimore.

[15] Ibid., 100, 101.

The news devastated the aspiring priest. "Augustine referred to this period in his life as a season of annealing. It was a year during which his faith was repeatedly subjected to the severest test, a year during which days and weeks of disillusionment and frustration at times drove him to the brink" of total despair — where his whole being seemed to be engulfed in impenetrable darkness.[16] But it was also an opportunity for gaining moral strength and courage that would prepare him well for life as the nation's first black priest.

In a last-ditch effort, Fr. Richardt wrote to the superior general of the Franciscan Order in Rome to make an appeal on Augustus's behalf. He "referred to Augustine as a reverent acolyte, a devoted son, a faithful worker, a diligent student, and a zealous lay apostle."[17] The report included a detailed description of Augustus's theological and spiritual formation to date, as well as an accurate account of the reasons Augustus was rejected by the seminaries in the United States.

Fr. Richardt's plan worked, and Augustus was accepted to the Urbanum Collegium de Propaganda Fide in Rome. He departed on February 15, 1880, and arrived March 12, the feast of Pope Gregory the Great, "one of the most determined enemies of slavery who ever sat in the Chair of Peter."[18]

Augustus was welcomed unconditionally and sincerely by the Vatican, not only as a seminarian, but also as a full member of the Church.

> For the first time in his life, Augustine sensed the sublime delight of the brotherhood of man under the fatherhood of God.... He experienced the security of equality and justice, a sense of dignity and worth, the comfort and

[16] Ibid., 122.
[17] Ibid.
[18] Ibid., 133.

companionship of friends, the joy of mutual charity and benevolence.... The oppressive weight of segregation was removed; the race barriers were gone. He never felt lonely, unwanted, or out of place. He was treated as a person ... as a child of God.[19]

Augustus thrived in the Eternal City, where his priestly vocation was nurtured and his gifts and talents were recognized, prompting the prefect of the Sacra Congregatio de Propaganda Fide to note what the American Church failed to appreciate: "Fr. Tolton is a good priest, reliable, worthy, and capable.... He is deeply spiritual and dedicated."[20]

After being ordained to the priesthood on April 24, 1886, Fr. Augustus Tolton toured England and Europe. He celebrated his first Mass in the United States for the School Sisters of Notre Dame. To this day, a plaque in the chapel of St. Mary's Hospital in Hoboken, New Jersey, reads: "The first Mass in the United States by the first Afro-American priest and ex-slave was celebrated on Wednesday, July 7, 1886." Fr. Tolton then celebrated his first solemn High Mass at St. Benedict the Moor Church, a black parish in New York City, on July 11, 1886, before a massive congregation. One week later, Fr. Tolton returned to Quincy, where he was soon installed as pastor of St. Joseph's parish, which served the black Catholics of Quincy.

He taught Bible history and catechism and instructed those seeking to enter the Church; he conducted counseling sessions, made home visits to the aged and sick, and recruited new parishioners. Fr. Tolton welcomed all, black and white, into his parish. The white members of his congregation were generous with their

---

[19] Ibid., 135.
[20] Ibid., 122.

financial and moral support for his work. Those who heard Fr. Tolton sensed the presence of the living Christ in him, and he developed a reputation as an outstanding preacher. Every Sunday, Mass at St. Joseph's was filled to capacity.

Despite these advances, the parish suffered instability caused by dire poverty and moral corruption, which had devastating effects on the black community. Many came to church only because the church was warm and they received shoes, clothes, and food. Infidelity and alcohol abuse were rampant. In addition, there were deliberate, systematic, and sustained attempts by Protestant denominations and "secret societies" to lure blacks away from the Catholic Church.

In one of the most painful episodes of Fr. Tolton's priesthood, he discovered that a white priest, Fr. Michael Weiss, had openly referred to him as the "nigger priest." Furthermore, Fr. Weiss insisted that white worshippers' contributions to St. Joseph's belonged to their own (white) parishes and that attendance at the black church was not valid for white Catholics. Despite their affection for Fr. Tolton, many white parishioners left St. Joseph's.

When Fr. Tolton's charitable attempts to reach an understanding with Fr. Weiss failed, Bishop James Ryan — who was a friend of Fr. Weiss — told him to minister to blacks only. The situation became so intolerable that Fr. Tolton appealed to Rome, requesting a transfer to another diocese. After a lengthy investigation, the Vatican approved his request. On December 7, 1889, Fr. Tolton received permission to transfer to the Archdiocese of Chicago after making an inquiry to Archbishop Patrick Feehan, who was thrilled to have Fr. Tolton among his priests. He left Quincy on December 19, believing he had been an utter disappointment to black Catholics there, and with the words "total failure," which had been suggested by some members of the white clergy, still ringing in his ears.

The Last Years

In Chicago, Fr. Tolton was appointed pastor of St. Augustine's Church, which was located in the basement of St. Mary's[21] and comprised blacks who were either barred from white parishes, were newcomers from the South, or were considering the Catholic Faith. Archbishop Feehan had complete confidence in Fr. Tolton, giving him full jurisdiction of all Negroes in Chicago.

However, as in Quincy, Fr. Tolton faced pressures both external and internal to the black community that were caused by segregation. The external factors included the racist attitudes of white priests and parishioners, and the aggressive proselytization of black Catholics by Protestant ministers. The internal factors included rampant poverty, substance abuse, economic instability, and moral squalor. As a result, Fr. Tolton received permission from Archbishop Feehan to open a temporary storefront mission (St. Monica Chapel) in the heart of Chicago's black district. Archbishop Feehan purchased the land and instructed Fr. Tolton to begin plans to build a real church. This required significant capital; the still-young priest knew this would be a daunting task given the neighborhood's prevailing economic circumstances. Most of the black population in the neighborhood was unemployed, transient, indolent, or isolated.

With the help of parishioners, Fr. Tolton embarked on an aggressive fund-raising campaign, to which he contributed from revenues received from speaking engagements throughout the United

[21] Built in the later 1860s, St. Mary's Catholic Church was located on the southeast corner of Ninth and Wabash in Chicago. When Holy Name Cathedral was destroyed by the Chicago fire just before its completion, St. Mary's became the temporary cathedral. On September 13, 1891, the *Chicago Times* wrote: "In Chicago the colored Catholic population is small and their needs are amply ministered to by Fr. Tolton (colored), in the basement of St. Mary's church on Wabash Ave."

States. He even appealed to Katharine Drexel, the famed educator who would later be canonized, for funds to build St. Monica's. He raised enough for construction to begin in 1891. In 1893, due to lack of funding, construction was halted and a temporary roof was installed, allowing the lower level of the church to be used for Mass and religious education. Fr. Augustus lived with his mother in the rectory behind the church, where she served as housekeeper and sacristan. Sadly, St. Monica's was never completed, and the parish was closed permanently in 1945.

Since moving to Chicago, Fr. Tolton had battled illness, and he grew weaker as he ignored his health and ministered unselfishly to the black community, helping to meet both their corporal and spiritual needs. The awesome responsibility for and obligation to the black Catholic community that Fr. Augustus carried on his shoulders and in his heart took its weighty toll, and on July 9, 1897, Fr. Augustus John Tolton died in Chicago of complications from heat stroke and uremia. He was forty-three years old. Fr. Tolton returned to Quincy, Illinois, one last time: to be buried in the priest's cemetery at St. Peter's.

Chapter 2

Overcoming Racism

The Church's Response

The inaugural Black Catholic Congress convened in 1889 at St. Augustine's parish in Washington, D.C. Fr. Tolton was the main celebrant and homilist at the opening Mass.

This was a major event for black Catholics; it included about a hundred delegates from all over the country, as well as members of the Catholic hierarchy and various Protestant ministers. President Grover Cleveland received the delegates at the White House, and Pope Leo XIII sent his blessing. The delegates issued a post-congress paper calling for Catholic schools, industrial education, admission to labor unions, and better housing for blacks. Four subsequent congresses met in northern cities through 1894, but the sixth congress did not convene until May 1987.[22]

In the ninety-three years between congresses, black Catholics continued to combat racism and discrimination within the Church. Slowly, American bishops began to speak out against

---

[22] Successive congresses have been held every five years since 1987, with the most recent, as of this writing, in Orlando, Florida, in 2018. More information on all Black Catholic Congresses can be found at the National Black Catholic Congress website: https://www.nbccongress.org/congresses.

racial inequality and its incompatibility with the Catholic Faith. Inspired by a letter from Pope Pius XII commemorating the 150th anniversary of the establishment of the American hierarchy, the United States bishops issued a document on World War II in which they stated that the

> rights of our minorities must be openly acknowledged and honestly respected. We ask this acknowledgment and respect particularly for our colored fellow citizens.... We fully appreciate their many native gifts and aptitudes, which, ennobled and enriched by a true Christian life, will make them a powerful influence in the establishment of a Christian social order.[23]

After the war, individual bishops took stands against segregation, especially in Catholic schools, and religious orders began accepting black candidates. Then, in the period immediately preceding the civil rights movement, the bishops issued the statement *Discrimination and Christian Conscience* (1958), saying:

> The heart of the race question is moral and religious. If our attitude is governed by the great Christian law of love of neighbor and respect for his rights, then we can work out harmoniously the technique of making legal, educational, economic, and social adjustments. But if our hearts are poisoned by hatred, or even by indifference toward the welfare and rights of our fellow men, then our nation faces grave internal crisis.[24]

---

[23] National Catholic Welfare Conference, "Black Catholics in the United States," *New York Age*, November 21, 1942, 12.

[24] United States Catholic Bishops, *Discrimination and Christian Conscience* (November 14, 1958), http://www.usccb.org/issues-

Overcoming Racism

There have been other statements on race from the sixties to the present day. In their pastoral letter *Brothers and Sisters to Us* (1979), the bishops stated:

Racism is an evil which endures in our society and in our Church. Despite apparent advances and even significant changes in the last two decades, the reality of racism remains. In large part, it is only external appearances which have changed. In 1958, we spoke out against the blatant forms of racism that divided people through discriminatory laws and enforced segregation. We pointed out the moral evil that denied human persons their dignity as children of God and their God-given rights. A decade later in a second pastoral letter we again underscored the continuing scandal of racism and called for decisive action to eradicate it from our society. We recognize and applaud the readiness of many Americans to make new strides forward in reducing and eliminating prejudice against minorities. We are convinced that the majority of Americans realize that racial discrimination is both unjust and unworthy of this nation.

Racism is a sin: a sin that divides the human family, blots out the image of God among specific members of that family, and violates the fundamental human dignity of those called to be children of the same Father. Racism is the sin that says some human beings are inherently superior and others essentially inferior because of race. It is the sin that makes racial characteristics the determining factor for the exercise of human rights. It mocks the

and-action/cultural-diversity/african-american/resources/upload/
Discrimination-Christian-Conscience-Nov-14-1958.pdf.

words of Jesus: "Treat the others the way you would have them treat you." Indeed, racism is more than a disregard for these words of Jesus; it is a denial of the truth of the dignity of each human being revealed by the mystery of the Incarnation.[25]

On September 9, 1984, the feast of St. Peter Claver, the ten black bishops of the United States at that time issued a groundbreaking document on evangelization and the black Catholic community called *What We Have Seen and Heard*. In that letter, the bishops wrote:

> Black people know what freedom is because we remember the dehumanizing force of slavery, racist prejudice and oppression. No one can understand so well the meaning of the proclamation that Christ has set us free than those who have experienced the denial of freedom. For us, therefore, freedom is a cherished gift. For its preservation, no sacrifice is too great. Hence, freedom brings responsibility. It must never be abused, equated with license nor taken for granted. Freedom is God's gift, and we are accountable to Him for our loss of it. And we are accountable for the gift of freedom in the lives of others. We oppose all oppression and all injustice, for unless *all* are free *none* are free.[26]

---

[25] United States Conference of Catholic Bishops (USCCB), *Brothers and Sisters to Us* (Washington: USCCB, 1979), http://www.usccb. org/issues-and-action/cultural-diversity/african-american/brothers-and-sisters-to-us.cfm.

[26] Joseph L. Howze, et al., *What We Have Seen and Heard: A Pastoral Letter on Evangelization from the Black Bishops of the United States* (September 9, 1984), http://www.usccb.org/issues-and-action/ cultural-diversity/african-american/resources/upload/what-we-have-seen-and-heard.pdf.

In recent years, individual bishops have also spoken openly about the issue of race. In 2015, in a response to a series of incidents involving African American men and law enforcement officials that sparked national outcry and protests, Louisville Archbishop Joseph E. Kurtz said:

> We mourn those tragic events in which African Americans and others have lost their lives in altercations with law enforcement officials.... In every instance, our prayer for every community is that of our Lord in St. John's Gospel, "that they all may be one." ... We join our voices with civic and religious leaders in pledging to work for healing and reconciliation. Our efforts must address root causes of these conflicts. A violent, sorrowful history of racial injustice, accompanied by a lack of educational, employment and housing opportunities, has destroyed communities and broken down families, especially those who live in distressed urban communities.[27]

Bishop Edward K. Braxton, shepherd of the Diocese of Bellville and an outspoken prelate on racism, stated in a lecture given at the Catholic University of America in 2017:

> We Catholics, like other Christians, sometimes have only a superficial cultural commitment to our faith. We do not experience our faith in Jesus Christ and his command to love at the deepest levels of our being. Only this deep existential commitment to follow Jesus as the Way, the Truth and the Life, will impel us to truly live the Catholic faith we profess in all of the complex and difficult situations of our lives,

---

[27] Archbishop Joseph E. Kurtz, Address to the Spring General Assembly of the United States Conference of Catholic Bishops, June 10, 2015, http://www.usccb.org/news/2015/15-088.cfm.

including those which will require us to oppose anyone and anything that serves to maintain the racial divide.[28]

Most recently, the United States Conference of Catholic Bishops established an ad hoc committee against racism. The committee, initiated by Cardinal Daniel N. DiNardo of Galveston-Houston, "will focus on addressing the sin of racism in our society, and even in our Church, and the urgent need to come together as a society to find solutions."[29] Cardinal DiNardo noted that "racism continues to afflict our nation" and that "the establishment of this new ad hoc committee will be wholly dedicated to engaging the Church and our society to work together in unity to challenge the sin of racism, to listen to persons who are suffering under this sin, and to come together in the love of Christ to know one another as brothers and sisters."[30] The cardinal continued:

> Prejudice can lurk unnoticed in the soul. Without prayerful reflection, it can feed on the fear of what is different. It can grow into overt racism. But self-reflection is not enough. It must lead to action.... The vile chants of violence against African Americans and other people of color, the Jewish people, immigrants, and others offend our faith, but unite our resolve. Let us not allow the forces of hate to deny the

---

[28] Most Reverend Edward K. Braxton Ph.D., S.T.D., "The Horizon of Possibilities: 'The Catholic Church and the Racial Divide in the United States: Old Wounds Reopened,'" address given at the Catholic University of America, Washington, D.C., October 23, 2017, http://www.diobelle.org/our-bishop/writings/1133-the-horizon-of-possibilities-the-catholic-church-and-the-racial-divide-in-the-united-states-old-wounds-reopened.

[29] USCCB, "U.S. Bishops Establish New Ad Hoc Committee Against Racism," USCCB, August 23, 2017, http://www.usccb.org/news/2017/17-149.cfm.

[30] Ibid.

intrinsic dignity of every human person. Let the nation and world see the one body of Christ move to the defense of our sisters and brothers who are threatened.[31]

In 1987, a year after the National Conference of Catholic Bishops established a standing committee for black Catholics, the Black Catholic Congress was reorganized as the National Black Catholic Congress (NBCC). The NBCC's mission is to establish an agenda for evangelization, to improve the spiritual, mental, and physical conditions of African Americans, and to work toward the full participation of black Catholics in the Church and in society. During the ensuing decades and into the twenty-first century, the NBCC has addressed a number of issues of concern to African American Catholics, including strengthening family values, spiritual enrichment, support for Catholic schools in black communities, and, more recently, AIDS, youth ministry, and faith formation.

The Image and Likeness of God

In the book of Genesis, God said, "'Let us make man in our image, after our likeness.' ... So God created man in His own image, in the image of God He created him; male and female He created them" (Gen. 1:26–27). Throughout history, sin has been a major obstacle to achieving true human freedom lived in God's image and likeness. The effect of sin through time is revealed in the experiences and attitudes of our "enlightened" culture, which manipulates truth and misuses freedom to such an extent that truth has become subjective and authentic freedom relative, looking both toward the self and away from the Creator. When

[31] Ibid.

combined with modernity's arrogant rejection of natural law, the cumulative effect obscures the vision of God in one another. As a consequence, some of what it means to be made in the image and likeness of God has been forgotten. "So often we try to deny this fact.... We know how to love, and yet we hate. We take the precious lives that God has given us and throw them away. We are unfaithful to those to whom we should be faithful. We are disloyal to those ideals to which we should be loyal. 'We are like sheep that have gone astray.' "[32]

Never was this truer in American history than during the turbulent Civil War era. In 1857 the Supreme Court ruled in *Dred Scott* that black people were property and not human beings. Chief Justice Taney, in his majority opinion, wrote, "[Slaves] had for more than a century before been regarded as beings of an inferior order, and altogether unfit to associate with the white race, either in social or political relations; and so far inferior, that they had no rights that the white man was bound to respect; and that the negro might justly and lawfully be reduced to slavery for his benefit." After citing the section of the Declaration of Independence about the equality of all men, Justice Taney adds insult to injury by stating, "It is too clear for dispute that the enslaved African race were not intended to be included.... The unhappy black race were separated from the white by indelible marks ... and were never thought of or spoken of except as property."[33] It was into this environment that

---

[32] Reverend Dr. Martin Luther King Jr., *The Measure of a Man* (Philadelphia: Christian Education Press, 1959), 10, 12.

[33] Compare this with the constant, unwavering position of the Magisterium of the Church, which has condemned slavery outright. Pope after pope, including Adrian I, Pius II, Eugene IV, Gregory XIV, Innocent XI, Benedict XIV, Pius VII, and many others, have strongly advocated against slavery, describing it as immoral, inhuman, and "the enemy of the human race." In 1537, 320 years before

the man who would become the first black priest in the United States came into the world.[34]

Dred Scott, Pope Paul III excommunicated those who enslaved the Indians of the Americas in his encyclical *Sublimus Dei*. For a comprehensive overview of the Catholic Church's official teaching on slavery, see Fr. Joel S. Panzer, *The Popes and Slavery* (New York: Alba House, 1996), and Mark Brumley, "Let My People Go: The Catholic Church and Slavery," *This Rock* (July–August 1999): 16–21. A number of Catholic Church antislavery documents in Latin were reprinted by Dr. Jaime Luciano Balmes, *El Protestantismo Comparado Con El Catolicismo* (Barcelona: Brusi, 1849), translated into English by C. J. Hanford and Robert Kershaw in *European Civilization: Protestantism and Catholicity Compared* (Baltimore: Murphy, 1850). Examples that Dr. Balmes cited include data from the following years: 441 (censuring slavers); 549 (church buildings as refuges for escaping slaves); 566 (excommunication-of-slavers proviso); 583 (Church issuance of freedom papers); 585 (use of Church property to free slaves); 595 (freeing entrants to monastic life); 616 (liberty-restoration proviso); 625 (banning new slaves; use of Church property to free current slaves); 666 (banning shaving slaves); 844 (use of Church property to free slaves); and 922 (defines slave trade as homicide).

[34] Three brothers of mixed blood preceded Fr. Tolton in the priesthood: James Augustine Healy (1830–1900), Patrick Francis Healy (1834–1910), and Alexander Sherwood Healy (1836–1875). Their father was an Irish immigrant and their mother a slave. The boys were taken from Georgia to Flushing, New York, where they attended a Quaker school. They were baptized later.

Bishop James Healy, valedictorian of Holy Cross College's first class, entered the Sulpician seminary in Montreal, was sent to study in Paris, and was ordained in Notre Dame Cathedral. He began his priestly duties in Boston, where few parishioners would accept him. He then served at a home for homeless boys, as secretary to the bishop, and as chancellor. Then he became pastor of one of Boston's largest parishes for nine years. In 1875 he was appointed bishop of Portland, Maine, where he became known as the "children's bishop." He served as bishop until he died some twenty-five years later. Under him, sixty-eight mission stations,

Fr. Augustus Tolton

What can we learn from the life and example of Fr. Tolton regarding racism? He was raised in an environment in which it was a common belief that "white people were superior to blacks and for that reason whites had the right or even the duty to dominate and control them and 'keep them in their place.'"[35] He and his family endured a lifetime of hatred and oppression both within and outside of the Church. Despite the fact that "from the time he was a small boy he learned, from an association with the white race, to accept the fact that degradation and contempt were the common lot of God's black children,"[36] Tolton never retaliated or sought revenge. Though he was upset by the circumstances of his time, his heart was never filled with animosity or vitriol. Instead, Augustus Tolton responded with love, patience,

---

eighteen parochial schools, and fifty churches were built. The Church recognized Bishop Healy's work by making him assistant to the papal throne, a rank just below that of cardinal.

Fr. Patrick Healy also went to Holy Cross. After studying at a Jesuit novitiate in Maryland and teaching at St. Joseph's College in Philadelphia, he returned to Holy Cross to teach and then to attend Georgetown University. He studied for the priesthood in Belgium, where he earned a Ph.D., believed to be another first for a black man. After the Civil War, he began teaching at Georgetown. He advanced to dean of studies, then acting president, and finally president in 1874. He introduced science courses, reorganized the schools of law and medicine, and beautified the campus. Prejudice apparently hampered his fund-raising efforts. The major building that he planned, built after he retired for health reasons, is named for him.

Fr. Sherwood Healy was ordained in Rome for the Boston Diocese in 1858. He served as rector of Holy Cross Cathedral in Boston from 1870 to 1875. Fr. Patrick apparently kept his racial origins secret; Fr. James did not hide his, but neither did he identify himself with the black community.

[35] Hemesath, *Slave to Priest*, 20.
[36] Ibid., 48.

and understanding. "He deplored the lack of spiritual guidance and opportunities ... open to ... blacks. Yet, he could understand why some white people were hostile, why many Catholics were indifferent, and why those in positions of authority in the Church sometimes vacillated."[37]

Encouraged by sympathetic and supportive priests, Augustus started working in the lay apostolate, becoming a successful catechist and evangelist to the black community in his adopted hometown of Quincy, Illinois. In the midst of the spiritual darkness and social turmoil that surrounded him, Augustus became the bright light and calming presence of Jesus Christ, and an untiring ambassador for the Catholic Faith. In imitation of Our Lord, who came down from Heaven "not to do my own will, but the will of him who sent me" (John 6:38), Augustus focused his attention not on himself but on the needs of all God's children. Filled with a profound spirit of humility and generosity, he worked diligently in the Lord's vineyard, becoming a living witness and example of the greatest commandments given to us by Christ: to love God and to love our neighbor as ourselves. "The silent, unobtrusive activity of Augustine Tolton was largely responsible for the success of the apostolate to the blacks of Quincy. Both he and his mother were tireless in their efforts to reinstate members of their race in the Church and to encourage others to study the Catholic religion."[38] Augustus knew that embracing the beauty and truth of the Catholic Faith in its fullness was the answer to the deplorable circumstances faced by those he served. "'Many of these people are Catholic,' thought Augustine. 'If they are sinners, they should have a chance to be

---

[37] Ibid., 101.
[38] Ibid., 100.

helped back to God. They could go to the sacraments and get their lives straightened out.' "[39]

Implications for Today

"Sooner or later, all the people of the world will have to discover a way to live together in peace, and thereby transform this pending cosmic elegy into a creative psalm of brotherhood."[40] The Reverend Dr. Martin Luther King Jr. spoke these striking words almost six decades ago when he accepted the Nobel Peace Prize. He went on to say that if peace and racial equality are to be achieved, "man must evolve for all human conflict a method which rejects revenge, aggression, and retaliation. The foundation of such a method is love."[41] Dr. King is speaking of a love rooted in faith, a faith that acknowledges that "God is love, and he who abides in love, abides in God and God abides in him" (1 John 4:16).

The key to defeating racism, in the spirit of Fr. Tolton, is to see our brothers and sisters as God sees us — to look at each other through God's eyes. We need to see the image and likeness of God in each other.

The word for "image" in Hebrew means a shadow that is the outline or representation of the original. When there is light, our physical bodies cast a shadow that is an outline of our bodies and that moves as we move. God is pure Spirit, and His light casts the shadow of His love on our souls. Just as our shadows move when we move, when we speak, think, and love, in cooperation with the light of grace in our souls, we reflect God's goodness in our actions.

---

[39] Ibid.

[40] Rev. Dr. Martin Luther King Jr., Nobel Prize acceptance speech, December 11, 1964.

[41] Ibid.

The word for "likeness" in Hebrew means "similar." "Likeness" in this context does not mean *physical* similarity. If I were situated between my son and a statue of myself, one might say they both resemble me; in fact, the statue would look more like me than my son would. Unlike the statue which is lifeless, my son and I, though separate individuals, share a common human nature composed of body and soul. Consequently, my son is much more in my likeness, in the sense used in Genesis, than the statue. Since God is pure Spirit, we bear a spiritual similarity to God, who has filled us with the breath of His divine life.

To begin defeating the scourge of racism in our world, three things need to happen: First, we need to be cognizant of the fact that racism is learned behavior, and that we can break down the walls of racism by taking a "hands-on" approach to creating an environment of mutual respect. We need to reach out with compassion to those of different races and hear their stories, respond with empathy, and work with humble, contrite hearts to build bridges of understanding in order to acknowledge the unique gifts we all bring to the Body of Christ.

Second, we need to see past stereotypes and, instead, see the image and likeness of God in each other. We should stop supporting media, individuals, and institutions that create, encourage, and perpetuate racist stereotypes. Racist ideologies create images that leave negative impressions on susceptible and vulnerable minds and hearts, especially those of children.

A shining example of seeing God in others in the spirit of Augustus Tolton was St. Teresa of Calcutta. Prior to her canonization, a number of secular media outlets aired stories about her life and work with the poorest of the poor. In one segment, a reporter followed Mother Teresa and her sisters for a day. They ministered to the poor and downtrodden on the streets of Calcutta who suffered from an array of terminal illnesses. The Sisters of Charity took loving care of these sons and daughters of God, bringing the homeless to their hospice, where they were cared for and eventually died with true dignity, surrounded by love and embraced by prayer. The reporter, however, noticed only the outward appearance of the people who were served: their repulsive stench, palsied limbs, and total vulnerability. The interviewer complained to the Saint of the Slums, "How can you be around people all day who look like this?" Mother Teresa looked at him quizzically and calmly responded, "Is that what they look like?" because when this great saint looked at someone, she saw Jesus.

Third, we should make sincere efforts to attend cultural events where the customs and traditions of other races can be appreciated and celebrated, not feared and caricatured. One of my roommates during freshman year had never been around African Americans before; when we first met in the room we were to share, he exclaimed, "You're black!" My heart sank a bit as I thought of how the year would unfold, but he ended up becoming one of my best friends.

The turning point came when I invited him to a dance sponsored by the Black Cultural Arts Club (BCAC). Most parties he had attended involved standing around and consuming large amounts of alcohol, so this experience of black culture—centered on fellowship and community, joyous, vibrant dance, and expressive language and gestures—was new to him. On the way back to the dorm, he could not stop talking about how much fun he had! This experience of a cultural celebration opened my roommate's mind and heart, leading to a number of substantive and meaningful conversations through which we both learned to appreciate and celebrate the gift of our differences, resulting in a friendship that has lasted to this day.

Fr. Tolton spent his life working to shatter racial barriers and facilitate dialogue in hopes of opening and broadening mutual understanding. His hope and prayer was that by his example of a life lived with spiritual integrity and wisdom, the Lord would use him as an instrument to bring about genuine, lasting change. Fr. Tolton hoped that his seminary experience in Rome would one day become the lived reality of every American: the experience of "equality and justice, a sense of dignity and worth, the comfort and companionship of friends, the joy of mutual charity and benevolence.... The oppressive weight of segregation was removed, the race barriers were gone. He never felt lonely, unwanted, or out of place. He was treated as a person, as a member of the Church, as a child of God."[42]

A Biblical Parallel: The Parable of the Good Samaritan

To understand the power of the parable of the good Samaritan (Luke 10:25–37), it is important to recognize the context in which Jesus tells it. First, a scholar of the law (an interpreter of the Mosaic law) tries to test Jesus by asking Him a question to which he already knew the answer: "Teacher, what shall I do to inherit eternal life?" Jesus does not fall for it and, employing a classic technique used by rabbis, answers the question with a question. In response, the lawyer answers his own question by quoting what Jesus would later call the greatest commandments: love God (Deut. 6:5) and love your neighbor as yourself (Lev. 19:18). Jesus is teaching the lawyer a moral lesson: that "love for our neighbor must accompany our love for God. These together, and not one without the other, are indispensable for living in God's friendship."[43] Jesus also makes

---

[42] Ibid., 135.

[43] *Ignatius Catholic Study Bible: New Testament*, Revised Standard Version, Second Catholic Edition, comp. Curtis Mitch, ed. Scott Hahn (San Francisco: Ignatius Press, 2010), 129.

the point that "holiness as defined by the Old Covenant is now surpassed by the holiness of the New."[44]

Anxious to justify himself, the scholar now asks for the meaning of the word "neighbor." For him "neighbor" meant only other Jews like himself—but did Jesus mean to include *every* Jew, even those who *did not* follow the Law? Was he supposed to love *them* also?

The trip from Jerusalem to Jericho is a seventeen-mile journey that ascends nearly 3,200 feet. "Its rough terrain made the roadway a target area for bandits and thieves."[45] In the parable, the priest and the Levite (roughly equivalent to a deacon today), who were expected to be lovers of God and neighbor, were probably walking in the other direction, heading toward the Temple in Jerusalem. They carefully passed by on the other side because the injured man would have been covered in blood; Israel's purity laws forbade them to touch the corpses of anyone other than family members (Lev. 21:1–3). They therefore chose to preserve their legal purity and so passed by the half-dead victim. In other words, they ignored the man for religious reasons and thought themselves justified under the law.

The Samaritan, in the eyes of the Jews, was an alien, an unwanted foreigner. There was longstanding hostility between the two neighboring peoples. The Samaritan was regarded as a half-breed, both physically and spiritually; Jews and Samaritans were ethnically related and shared some religious beliefs, but the Samaritans were seen as heretics. In fact, they were held in such contempt by the Jews that, in answer to Jesus' question about which of the three was a neighbor to the man who was robbed and beaten, the lawyer could not bring himself to say, "The Samaritan," but only, "The one who showed him mercy."

---

[44] Ibid.
[45] Ibid.

Yet, this despised outsider—presumed to have nothing of the spirit of God's mercy and compassion—gives the Jew lying on the ground the attention that the Jewish clergymen refused to give. In fact, the Samaritan went to extraordinary lengths to take care of the injured man, sparing no expense. The two denarii (silver coins) that the Samaritan spent on him may not seem like very much to us today, but it represented two days' wages and would have been enough to take care of several days' lodging for the man.

What would you do in that situation? It is easy to say, "I would help the guy." What if the almost dead man was the one who made racist comments about Sebastian de la Cruz, the Mexican-American boy who sang the national anthem at the NBA finals in 2013?[46] What if the man lying on the ground was the one who said, "This little Mexican snuck in the country like four hours ago and now he's singing the anthem," or, "Can't believe they had the nerve to have a beaner singing the anthem of America."

What if he was the person who assaulted you? What if he was the person who got you hooked on drugs or alcohol or pornography? What if he was the person who molested you as a child? The person who drove drunk and killed your spouse? As we walked by him on the side of the road, the anger and hatred we would feel would burn like a fire in our hearts, and we would want—more than anything—for the person who hurt us to suffer greatly, even to the point of death. We would want to leave him lying there and say, "You deserve it!" and not give him a second thought.

---

[46] See David Knowles, "Mexican-American Boy, Sebastien de la Cruz, Sings Encore Performance of National Anthem at NBA Finals in Response to Bigoted Comments," *Daily News*, June 14, 2013, http://www.nydailynews.com/news/national/mexican-american-boy-national-anthem-performance-sparks-racist-backlash-article-1.1371990.

Fr. Augustus Tolton

Yet, Our Lord calls us to do the seemingly impossible: He tells us that we must be Good Samaritans. "The Samaritan exemplifies a new standard of holiness, where God no longer requires his people to separate from others, but calls them to extend mercy to everyone in need and to exclude no one on the grounds of prejudice" or hatred. [47] Our Lord gives us no other options and makes no exceptions. Jesus knows the human heart, and when our hearts are angry and bitter and full of resentment (even though it may be justified) there is a part of us that is imprisoned by hate—a hate that can diminish or even block being open to forgiveness from others and receiving forgiveness from God.

The parable of the good Samaritan tells the story of our salvation and shows us the way to overcome racial divisions. Adam, who represents the fullness of humanity in Genesis, "is the man attacked by Satan and his legions; he is stripped of his immortality and left dead in sin. The priest and the Levite represent the Old Covenant and its inability to restore man to new life. Jesus Christ comes as the Good Samaritan to rescue man from death and bring him to the inn of the Church for [spiritual] refreshment and healing through the sacraments."[48] Our Lord tells us that we must love our enemies and that, if we are truly His disciples, we must pick up our cross daily and follow Him. Christ, in the parable of the good Samaritan, reveals the love and mercy of God and demands that Christians be guided in their lives by love and mercy toward their neighbor.[49] "Believing in the crucified Son means 'seeing the Father'; means believing that love is present in the world and that this love is more powerful than any kind of evil in which

[47] *Ignatius Catholic Study Bible*, 129.
[48] Ibid.
[49] See Pope John Paul II, Encyclical Letter *Dives in Misericordia* (*Rich in Mercy*) (November 30, 1980), no. 3.

individuals, humanity, or the world are involved. Believing in this love means believing in mercy."[50]

Who is the person you have written off and left for dead at the roadside of your life? Who is the person in your life who does not know the love and mercy of God? Mercy and forgiveness demonstrate the presence in the world of a love that is more powerful than sin.[51] With the example of Fr. Tolton to inspire and challenge us, let us lovingly accept Our Lord's invitation to discipleship, to "go and do likewise" (Luke 10:37), as living signs and witnesses of God's tender love and mercy, so that the world may see the good work that we do and give glory to God.

[50] Ibid., no. 7.
[51] Ibid., no. 14.

Chapter 3

Building Strong Families

From 1974 through 1979, the groundbreaking sit-com *Good Times* aired on CBS. *Good Times* followed the challenges and joys of the close-knit Evans family, who lived in a housing project in inner-city Chicago. The episodes were usually uplifting and positive as television audiences around the country watched the Evans family struggle and persevere together.

The Evans family represented the undaunted determination of so many black families throughout the postwar and Jim Crow eras—and into the period of the civil rights movement—as they fought to reunite and rebuild. James and Florida Evans epitomized a long tradition of black parents striving to open doors for their children, creating opportunities for them to succeed, despite the seemingly insurmountable barriers of racial oppression and poverty. "Black families strove to lift a veil of ignorance from a society that held them down, condemned them to slavery, and denied them educational opportunities, thus limiting them to working as unskilled, cheap laborers."[52] Yet, in the face

---

[52] See Juan William on Cosby in Juan Williams, *Enough: The Phony Leaders, Dead-End Movements, and Culture of Failure That Are Undermining Black America—and What We Can Do about It* (New

of tremendous adversity, black families struggled, prayed, and remained together.

Challenges to Family Life

What does it mean to be a family in today's society? What does contemporary culture say to families about truth, faith, and the meaning of life? These questions can be answered by simply watching most movies, music videos, and television shows, or by reading news stories in secular and social media. They flood us with pointless anecdotes, half-truths, and fly-by-night morality. This type of thinking will ultimately lead to a collapse of truth and integrity and, ultimately, to the destruction of our Christian heritage.

We are already seeing signs of this. Family members seem more comfortable texting one another rather than talking. "Quality family time" centers on the children's sporting events or other social activities, and not family nights at home, when parents and siblings simply enjoy being with each other. Moreover, many families experience some form of "secular creep," in which Mass attendance, catechetical instruction, and even family prayer take a back seat to worldly endeavors. The pressure of managing a work-life balance often creates palpable tension in the home, particularly when a spouse feels neglected. Immediate self-gratification takes precedence over chastity, discipline, and self-control as evidenced by cyberbullying and the pornography pandemic that is destroying families.

Through euthanasia and abortion, the inherent dignity of men, women, and children is all but forgotten, and what self-respect remains is exploited for superficial pleasure by the malevolent

York: Crown Publishers, 2006), 4, http://www.cbsnews.com/htdocs/pdf/Enough_excerpt.pdf.

human-trafficking industry. Society is attempting to systematically redefine the God-given institution of marriage and actively promotes an ideology that seeks to decouple gender entirely from sex. Domestic abuse and other forms of senseless violence have reached epidemic proportions.

Unlike today, when many families labor under the oppressive weight of moral relativism and secularism, the Tolton family experienced incomprehensible hardship and cruelty under the oppressive regime of slavery. Peter Paul and Martha Jane Tolton — the parents of the future priest — were treated as subhuman from the beginning of their marriage. "The respective owners of the couple consented to the marriage under this agreement: the Toltons would live in a cabin on the Eliot farm, and Peter would remain a slave of the Hager family. All children born of the union would be the property of Stephen Eliot."[53]

For the sake of their children, the Toltons were determined to be liberated from the tyranny of the slave trade. Mr. Tolton could not bear the thought of his three children growing up as slaves, so he resolved to fight for his family's freedom in the ongoing war. His motive was clear: "I'll save my earnings and come back to you and the children when the war is over," he told Martha Jane. "They must be free. They must learn to read and write; they must go to school and to church; they must have freedom."[54] With the full support and encouragement of his wife, Peter Paul, "strengthened by her faith and love … tore himself away from his dear ones" and joined the northern army.[55]

He never came home.

Are we as determined to fight for our family?

[53] Hemesath, *Slave to Priest*, 27.
[54] Ibid., 29.
[55] Ibid.

In the face of these challenges, we must work diligently—as Fr. Tolton and his parents did—to protect and defend the dignity of the family. We must develop a spirituality within the family that witnesses to the truth that God is love, that He calls all families to live in personal loving communion with Him, and that love is not simply a "feeling" but a participation in the self-giving and life-giving love of the three Persons of the Trinity: Father, Son, and Holy Spirit.

The relational nature of God is revealed to us most fully in Jesus Christ, who "restore(s) the unity of all in one people and one body."[56] This unity is expressed in a special way through the family, which forms a community of persons and "is thus the first human 'society.' It arises whenever there comes into being the covenant of marriage, which opens the spouses to a lasting communion of love and of life, and it is brought to completion in a full and specific way with the procreation of children: the 'communion' of the spouses gives rise to the 'community' of the family."[57] Together, the married couple forms a lifelong,[58] self-donating, and unbreakable

---

[56] *Catechism of the Catholic Church* (CCC), no. 813, quoting *Gaudium et Spes* 78 § 3. This paragraph adds: "It is the Holy Spirit, dwelling in those who believe and pervading and ruling over the entire Church, who brings about that wonderful communion of the faithful and joins them together so intimately in Christ that he is the principle of the Church's unity." Ibid., quoting *Unitatis Redintegratio* 2 § 2.

[57] Pope John Paul II, *Letter to Families* (February 2, 1994), no. 7.

[58] "The sacrament of Matrimony can be regarded in two ways: first in the making and then in its permanent state. For it is a sacrament like to that of the Eucharist, which not only while it is being conferred, but also while it remains, is a sacrament; for as long as the married parties are alive, so long is their union a sacrament of Christ and his Church." Pius XI, *Casti Connubii* (December 31, 1930), no. 110.

union of love: a "communion of persons intended to bear witness on earth and to image the intimate communion of persons within the Trinity."[59] In other words, since God exists as a "family" of Persons and we are made in the "image and likeness of God," the family on earth reflects the family of divine Persons in Heaven, which we call the Holy Trinity.

The Church is the Body of Christ, and just as Christ loves the Church, so husbands and wives must love each other (Eph. 5:21–31). This relationship of love, life, intimacy, and communion was exemplified in the matrimonial covenant that Peter Paul and Martha Jane Tolton so beautifully shared. As the domestic church—that is, the church of the home—reflects the universal Church, so the love of spouses reflects the love of Christ for His Church. This reality is not possible in its fullness without the Eucharist, which, within the lasting bond of sacramental Matrimony, nourishes the spouses' union, renews their strength, and makes their communion deeper and more real. This is the faith that sustained the Tolton family and heavily influenced the priestly ministry of Fr. Tolton, who dedicated much of his life to strengthening families.

What was true for the Tolton family in the nineteenth century remains true for us in the twenty-first: The family needs the nourishment of the Eucharist to survive. The Eucharist is Christ Himself; it is the fountain from which we receive the strength, power, and grace to seek the Lord by living holy lives and by participating in works of justice and charity.

Through the deepening of family spirituality and prayer life, through the strengthening of our efforts to image Christ within us, and by contemplating the Eucharist and its relationship to the

---

[59] William E. May, *Marriage: The Rock on Which the Family Is Built* (San Francisco: Ignatius Press, 1995), 65.

covenant of Matrimony, our families will be greatly enriched as they reflect the love of Christ present both in the Church and in one another throughout their lives.

The Role of Parents

Every one then who hears these words of mine and does them will be like a wise man who built his house upon the rock; and the rain fell, and the floods came, and the winds blew and beat upon that house, but it did not fall, because it had been founded on the rock. And every one who hears these words of mine and does not do them will be like a foolish man who built his house upon the sand; and the rain fell, and the floods came, and the winds blew and beat against that house, and it fell; and great was the fall of it. (Matt. 7:24–27)

Fr. Tolton learned this invaluable lesson from his family: It is parents' job to lay in the lives of their children a strong foundation upon which they can build a deep, lasting faith — not to build the house of their lives for them. Our children must cooperate with the will of God and build the house of their lives with the Lord.[60] This truth was the driving force behind Fr. Tolton's approach to evangelization — to lead by example, to be the hands and feet of Christ to those he served: "The children must hear us say the prayers and the catechism and watch us do things like going to church and see how Mass is celebrated and how we do things in church. They must watch us receive Holy Communion and go to confession. They have to hear the priest read the Epistles and the

---

[60] "If the Lord does not build the house, in vain do its builders labor" (Ps. 127:1).

Gospels and listen to the sermons and instructions. That is the way they will learn."[61]

There is an interesting parallel between contemporary parents and the slave families of Fr. Tolton's time. Both were and are, for the most part, ill-equipped to teach their children the Faith. The parents of slaves were both illiterate and uneducated, the result of a shared general belief at the time that "white people were superior to blacks and for that reason whites had the right or even the duty to dominate and control them [and] to keep the slaves illiterate [since] the ability to read and write could endanger the whole system of servitude."[62] Parents today are, for the most part, poorly catechized themselves and simply do not know and cannot articulate even the basic truths of the Faith, never mind living that Faith at home as exemplars for their children. Thus, in both cases but for very different reasons, parents have outsourced their responsibility, leaving the critical task of primary evangelization to Catholic schools and parish youth groups, whose main role and purpose is to *support* and *supplement*—not take the place of—the role of parents in the domestic church:

> Education in the faith by the parents should begin in the child's earliest years. This already happens when family members help one another to grow in faith by the witness of a Christian life in keeping with the Gospel. Family catechesis precedes, accompanies, and enriches other forms of instruction in the faith. Parents have the mission of teaching their children to pray and to discover their vocation as children of God. The parish is the Eucharistic community and the heart of the liturgical life of Christian families;

[61] Hemesath, *Slave to Priest*, 97.
[62] Ibid., 20.

it is a privileged place for the catechesis of children and parents.[63]

What three things can mothers and fathers do to strengthen their families and help get their children to Heaven?

First , understand that the grace of the sacrament of Matrimony assists parents in fulfilling the responsibility and privilege of evangelizing their children. While Father Tolton lost his own father at a young age and, of course, had no biological children of his own, he lived out the vocation of a father in his role as a priest. Augustus Tolton, first as a lay catechist and then as a pastor, cherished his role as spiritual father to these children. He "kept bringing in more and more children and helped them with their prayers and catechism."[64] He used funds that were collected for the building of his parish in Chicago "for food, medicine, clothes, and adequate shelter … to alleviate the sufferings of poverty-stricken families" while teaching "Christian doctrine after both Masses on Sunday."[65] This holy priest shows us that evangelization is not only about teaching and catechizing; for the Good News to be both effective and life-changing, it must move the mind and the heart so that those who hear and experience the Way, the Truth, and the Life through us will fall in love with Jesus. "You are the light of the world.… Let your light shine before men, that they may see your good works and give glory to your Father who is in heaven" (Matt. 5:14, 16). Fr. Tolton embodied Christ's words to the fullest and gave an example for all families to follow.

[63] CCC 2226; cf. LG 11.
[64] Hemesath, *Slave to Priest*, 99.
[65] Ibid., 210.

Parents may ask themselves, "Why am *I* called to evangelize? We're so busy, and life is hectic enough as it is. We are doing our best!" We can never forget that the ultimate goal of mothers and fathers is to help get each other and their children to Heaven, which is what it means to live out the primary purposes of marriage: the good of the spouses, and the bearing and education of children. Therefore, as the Tolton family shows us, parents are the first evangelizers and witnesses of the Faith to their children. But the Faith cannot take hold in children's hearts if it is not first rooted in the hearts of their parents; you simply cannot give what you do not have yourself.

Faith is a gift from God that we first received in Baptism. The gift of grace in Baptism is completed and strengthened in the sacrament of Confirmation, and is nurtured by Christ's Body, Blood, Soul, and Divinity in the Eucharist. "Grace is favor, the free and undeserved help that God gives us to respond to his call to become children of God, adoptive sons, partakers of the divine nature and of eternal life. Grace is a participation in the life of God. It introduces us into the intimacy of Trinitarian life: by Baptism the Christian participates in the grace of Christ."[66]

Baptism and Confirmation leave an indelible mark on our souls, "which is the sign that Jesus Christ has marked a Christian with the seal of his Spirit by clothing him with power from on high so that he may be his witness."[67] The sacraments, however, are not magic. They have power in our lives only when we freely cooperate with what God wants to do in us through His grace: "You, therefore, must be perfect, as your heavenly Father is perfect" (Matt. 5:48). This does not mean that we are without fault or error. We are called to a perfect—that is, a mature, fully grown, and complete—life

[66] CCC 1996, 1997.
[67] CCC 1304.

in Jesus. It is this life imbued with deep faith that we hand down to our children and that provides the steel pilings that support the foundation of our children's lives.

By their Baptism into Christ's death, parents are called to model discipleship to their children. A disciple is one who hears, accepts, and carries out the teachings of Jesus Christ and His Church in his or her life every day. A disciple follows and imitates Jesus. Each of us who has been baptized has this mission and calling: to actively share our experience of knowing Jesus Christ personally and then to invite others to share in His life!

Second, "parents have the first responsibility for the education of their children. They bear witness to this responsibility first by creating a home where tenderness, forgiveness, respect, fidelity, and disinterested service are the rule.... Parents should teach their children to subordinate the 'material and instinctual dimensions to interior and spiritual ones.' Parents have a grave responsibility to give good example to their children."[68] The education spoken of here is distinct from (though, of course, related to) the Christian duty to evangelize our children, as described above.

After Peter Paul's death, Martha Jane Tolton assumed this responsibility with tremendous courage and with the help of God's grace. "Although illiterate, she knew the Ten Commandments and she taught her family how to observe them. Prayers she had learned as a slave were said regularly every day with the added incentive: 'We must never forget to thank the Lord for his goodness, and we must ask him to take care of us always.' ... 'I learned my praying and my singing at my mother's knee,' was Augustine's lifelong boast."[69]

---

[68] CCC 2223.
[69] Hemesath, *Slave to Priest*, 38–39.

My father, who was not a man of faith while my siblings and I were growing up, did not teach me how to be man. I relied on the witness and example of other men in my life who helped shape me into the man I am today. I did not want this to be the case with my son and so, shortly after his twelfth birthday, I began taking him on what I call Guys Nights Out. At first, we discussed the physical changes of puberty that were beginning to manifest in his adolescent body, but, as time went on, we broadened the discussion to include topics that would seriously impact the formation of his moral conscience: the redefinition of marriage, abortion, euthanasia, pornography, human trafficking, transgenderism, and other relevant issues. Just as Peter Paul Tolton gave his life to free his children from the physical bonds of slavery, parents must give their lives—their time and attention—to free their children from the intellectual bonds of moral relativism and secular humanism.

"The home is well suited for education in the virtues. This requires an apprenticeship in self-denial, sound judgment, and self-mastery—the preconditions of all true freedom."[70] This is a critically important issue for parents. Tragically, many young people today do not have the ability to reason logically, nor do they desire to engage in rational discourse with someone who has an opposing viewpoint. Rather, they allow their emotions to take center stage and are easily offended when someone offers a differing opinion. Many college and university campuses, instead of being places of scholarly engagement and the rigorous exchange of ideas, have treated their students like children, creating "safe spaces" where students who are offended by disquieting ideas can go and feel safe. Thus, instead of creating an environment where difficult issues can be discussed openly while respecting the dignity of everyone involved, institutions of higher education are

[70] CCC 2223.

now champions of censorship and the suppression of free speech, engendering the very intolerance they claim to be combating. This way of thinking is the antithesis of the Catholic intellectual and moral tradition, particularly with regard to the meaning of freedom.

As I wrote in a previous book:

> Our culture tells us that freedom means "independence" — that I don't need to subject myself to principles that are true in themselves but that truth can be changed to fit popular trends or my particular situation. John the Apostle, the disciple whom Jesus loved, reminds us that man's deepest truth and identity is to be in God: "God is love, and he who abides in love abides in God, and God abides in him" (John 4:16). The truth of God's ever abundant and merciful love is rooted in authentic freedom, a freedom "from" and a freedom "for": the freedom from sin so that we can be free for God.[71]

This freedom is developed by the practice of virtue. "A virtue is a habitual and firm disposition to do the good. It allows the person not only to perform good acts, but to give the best of himself.... He pursues the good and chooses it in concrete actions."[72]

Virtuous habits take long hours of practice. When our free will cooperates with the time and effort necessary to build virtue (that is, when we freely choose to align ourselves with the objective, transcendent principles of the natural law), living virtuously becomes a joyful experience. If free will, however, does not cooperate with the development of virtue (that is, when we freely choose

---

[71] Deacon Harold Burke-Sivers, *Behold the Man: A Catholic Vision of Male Spirituality* (San Francisco: Ignatius Press, 2015), 73.
[72] CCC 1803.

to align ourselves with the subjective, worldly principles of radical individualism), we become enslaved to our passions, feelings, and emotions. It becomes increasingly difficult to move ourselves beyond this way of thinking, and we ultimately become unhappy. We want to have individuality and uniqueness, but we find out quickly that true uniqueness can occur only if it is rooted in the deep soil and core principles of the natural moral law.

This is why, for example, we can hear twenty piano virtuosos play the same concerto note for note, yet each sounds different: The individuality of each musician shows through in how he or she interprets the music. The common thread is that they all started out by agreeing to master the objective principles that control how music works. Thus, it is only on a foundation of such principles that we can build true uniqueness; individuality must be rooted in something that is true and, thus, shared. St. John Paul II summarizes this point beautifully:

> The separation which some have posited between the freedom of individuals and the nature which all have in common … obscures the perception of the universality of the moral law on the part of reason. But inasmuch as the natural law expresses the dignity of the human person and lays the foundation for his fundamental rights and duties, it is universal in its precepts and its authority extends to all mankind. *This universality does not ignore the individuality of human beings*, nor is it opposed to the absolute uniqueness of each person. On the contrary, it embraces at its root each of the person's free acts, which are meant to bear witness to the universality of the true good. By submitting to the common law, our acts build up the true communion of persons and, by God's grace, practise charity, "which binds everything together in perfect harmony" (Col. 3:14). When on the contrary they disregard

the law, or even are merely ignorant of it, whether culpably or not, our acts damage the communion of persons, to the detriment of each.[73]

Fr. Tolton's formation experiences—starting at home with his mother and father (spiritual and human formation) and continuing with his private tutoring (intellectual formation), his work in the lay apostolate (pastoral formation), and his seminary training at the Vatican (spiritual, human, intellectual, and pastoral formation)—freed him to be a man of great virtue. He was "distinguished for his exemplary life. Everyone admired his daily little acts of goodness that showed his worth and the larger virtues that revealed his character. Augustine's spiritual life was deepened and his knowledge of religion was enriched."[74] By freely cooperating with the transcendent principles of the natural law and the grace of the sacraments, Augustus Tolton became the man God created him to be—and the first black priest in the United States.

Parents can help instill virtuous behavior into their children in three ways that can be a part of daily family life:

1. Help them develop the habit of making good choices to build spiritual muscle memory. As practice and repetition perfect an athlete's skills, living a life of virtue builds spiritual muscle memory so that living our faith in the world becomes second nature. Faith, then, becomes not just "what we do" but "who we are," influencing all our action and decisions.

2. Teach children to fight the lure of sin and disordered desires by asking God and the Blessed Mother to help them. They should start praying the Our Father and

---

[73] John Paul II, Encyclical Letter *Veritatis Splendor* (*The Splendor of Truth*) (August 6, 1993), no. 51.

[74] Hemesath, *Slave to Priest*, 139.

the Hail Mary during times of temptation, and ask Jesus and Mary to be with them in those moments. Praying the St. Michael Prayer and asking for the intercession of saints (especially their Confirmation saints) are also very helpful.

3. Teach children to seek God's grace regularly in the sacraments of Reconciliation and the Eucharist, and to cooperate with God's grace. One especially important way we can nurture that cooperation with grace is to encourage them to learn as much as they can about *why* the Church teaches what She does and *how* the Faith connects with their everyday experience.

Advancement in virtue is the foundation for educating our children. When confronted by the high priest for speaking the truth in love, "Peter and the apostles answered, 'We must obey God rather than men'" (Acts 5:29). St. Paul teaches, "Do not be conformed to this world but be transformed by the renewal of your mind, that you may prove what is the will of God, what is good and acceptable and perfect" (Rom. 12:2). Jesus said, "If you continue in my word, you are truly my disciples, and you will know the truth, and the truth will make you free" (John 8:31–32). In short, parents must model for their children what it means to love God with all our heart, with all our soul, with all our mind, and with all our strength. These profound, timeless principles of Catholic life, when practiced with fidelity in the home, will open the door to endless possibilities for families today, as they did for Fr. Tolton in his day. "Diligent study and daily discipline molded Augustine into a man of stability, a man of moral strength and courage."[75] Stability. Moral strength. Courage. These are virtues that any parents would want for their children.

[75] Ibid., 140.

A third thing that mothers and fathers can do to strengthen their families and help get their children to Heaven is to live "eucharistically." This means taking the experience of Jesus at Mass, in Word and sacrament, and applying it to family life. Here are four practical suggestions for doing this in your family:

1. Have a family night for one hour, once a week, when everyone in the family participates in a common activity (that does not involve watching television). This could involve physical activities, such as walking in the park or riding bikes, playing board games, or even attending a fun activity at the parish. Family night should always end with prayer.

2. Husbands and wives should go on a date night at least once a month. Get a babysitter (or two!) to watch the kids and enjoy an evening out — just the two of you. Use that time not only to have fun but to talk about how things are going between the two of you. Sometimes parents can get so busy managing the household (the mortgage and the utilities, home projects, and children's activities) that they rarely spend any time nurturing their marriage covenant. Spending quality time together will both strengthen your marriage and be a great witness to your children of your love and affection toward each other.

3. Engage in corporal works of mercy. Volunteer as a family at your parish St. Vincent de Paul conference, or at a local homeless shelter or soup kitchen. Offer to deliver Thanksgiving dinner or Christmas food boxes to homebound parishioners or other families in need. In a culture that promotes individualism and in which many young

people have a warped sense of entitlement, children need to see that the world is much bigger than they are and that true joy in life comes from being a gift to others. Parents can teach their children that it is when you give yourself away in love that you truly find yourself in God.

4. Attend Mass together every week and Eucharistic Adoration at least one hour a week. You can teach children the concept of the Eucharist by taking them to Mass and, at the elevation of the Host at the Consecration, simply saying, "There's Jesus." The key is to connect what is happening at Mass to their lives. Another way to make this connection is by reading the Sunday Gospel at the dinner table during the week and talking about it: What is Jesus saying? Why is it important? What does this teaching have to do with my life?

Attending Adoration teaches children how to listen to God's voice. One way to get children comfortable with the concept of Adoration is to have them spend a few minutes in silence each day. For example, when the kids come home from school and before they have a snack or start their homework, have them spend five or ten minutes in their rooms in silence. The parents' example of going to Adoration will teach their children how to listen to God in their hearts, how to appreciate that quiet time nurtures a personal relationship with God, and that silence allows God's voice to change their lives.

Building a strong family centered on the love of God is not always easy; it takes a lot of work. But know that from the day of your wedding until death you have God's grace to help you through the most difficult times and the toughest challenges, for with God all things are possible! Always remember that He is the fountain from which you and your spouse will receive the strength, power, and grace you need to help each other (and your children) get to Heaven.

Fr. Augustus Tolton

The Role of Husbands and Fathers

Why do so many men view women as nothing more than possessions to be discarded when they are no longer useful or no longer hold their interest? Why have too many men bought into the lie that love does not mean commitment, self-gift, and sacrifice?

> There exists an entire generation of fathers who have physically, emotionally or spiritually abandoned their wives and children. Thus, in the absence of fathers to lead, support and nurture their families, women have compensated either by assuming masculine roles within the family, or by constructing innovative support networks for themselves and their children. This changing dynamic has brought us to a critical juncture as men: we are at the genesis of a systemic and fundamental shift in family life where in the near future, if we continue to live as men of the culture, fathers in the family may be considered optional and, in many cases, unnecessary.[76]

In a 1987 address to a meeting of black Catholics in the United States, Pope St. John Paul II said that men "must rediscover the spirit of family life, which refuses to be destroyed in the face of even the most oppressive forces" affecting society.[77] Husbands and wives must stand with the Church in defending the rights of families and in teaching by their example "the obligations and responsibilities [of family life] which lead to the fullness of joy and life."[78]

Peter Paul Tolton was a shining example of authentic fatherhood, sacrificing his life for his family. He and his wife were one

---

[76] Burke-Sivers, *Behold the Man*, 5.
[77] Pope John Paul II, Meeting with the black Catholics of New Orleans (September 12, 1987), no. 4.
[78] Ibid.

flesh, and Mrs. Tolton never let her children forget the gift of their father's love and devotion to them. She would regularly "recite the story of their father, his courage and bravery. 'He was so good and kind.... He said he would make the world a better place to live in.' ... He said, 'I will fight for them, make us all free, and then come back home.'"[79] Peter Paul Tolton's life would have a profound effect upon his son, who, through a life of prayer, faith, and perseverance, would see his father's dream come to fruition.

As the father of three daughters, I know the day is coming when young men will arrive at my home to take my daughters on dates. This is one of the reasons I have taken the initiative to have each daughter experience her first "date" with me. I understand that when they walk out the door on real dates, each young woman will be taking with her the same experience they will take down the aisle or into the convent one day: years of watching how I treat my wife, her mother. The greatest gift I could ever give my children is to die to myself every day and to live for them. "Husbands, love your wives, as Christ loved the Church and gave himself up for her" (Eph. 5:25). "A husband's mission is to imitate the crucified Christ, to give his life and die every day to himself through acts of sacrificial love and service so that he can live for his wife and children, just as Christ the Bridegroom gave His life for His Bride, the Church."[80] If I want my daughters to marry the men of their dreams, I'd better show them what one looks like!

Peter Paul Tolton taught Augustus from an early age that "every man is called to be the chief servant of his family, whether he serves as a husband and father in the domestic church (the church of the home), as a parish priest *in persona Christi* (in the person of Christ)

---

[79] Hemesath, *Slave to Priest*, 36.
[80] Burke-Sivers, *Behold the Man*, 34.

for the Church on earth, or as a young man who serves as an example of sanctity and virtue within society as he discerns God's will for his life."[81] Peter Paul prepared the future priest to meet life's challenges head-on with courage, conviction, and humility, just as the greatest king in the history of Israel, David, before he died, prepared his son Solomon to assume the role of king. In his last moments on earth, David did not tell his son how to defeat his enemies, how to be popular and loved by the people, or how to accumulate wealth. Instead, David told Solomon that he must be a man. But he didn't stop there. He went on to tell his son how he must be a *man of God*:

> I am about to go the way of all the earth. Be strong, and show yourself a man, and keep the charge of the LORD your God, walking in his ways and keeping his statutes, his commandments, his ordinances, and his testimonies, as it is written in the law of Moses, that you may prosper in all that you do and wherever you turn; that the LORD may establish his word which he spoke concerning me, saying, "If your sons take heed to their way, to walk before me in faithfulness with all their heart and with all their soul, there shall not fail you a man on the throne of Israel." (1 Kings 2:2–4)

King David and Peter Paul Tolton personify what every father, every priest, and every man who mentors the next generation can and must do: prepare our sons for spiritual battle! Like David, Peter Paul, by the witness and example of his life, told Augustus that if he followed the law of the Lord and put the Lord first in his life, he would prosper, and that if he became a living example of fidelity and holiness, future generations of men would not fail in their mission to serve, protect, and defend God's people. If men are to

[81] Ibid., 35.

thrive in today's society and become beacons of hope, light, and strength in a culture of despair, darkness, and death, we must be equipped to face Satan as if our lives and eternal salvation depended on it. "Peter Paul Tolton lay buried, unknown and unsung ... but the memory of him—his purpose in life and the price he paid to reach his goal—lay enshrined in the heart of his son, a courageous ideal to live up to."[82]

The Role of Wives and Mothers

Motherhood implies from the beginning a special openness to the new person: and this is precisely the woman's "part". In this openness, in conceiving and giving birth to a child, the woman "discovers herself through a sincere gift of self". The gift of interior readiness to accept the child and bring it into the world is linked to the marriage union, which should constitute a special moment in the mutual self-giving both by the woman and the man. According to the Bible, the conception and birth of a new human being are accompanied by the following words of the woman: *"I have brought a man into being with the help of the Lord"* (Gen. 4:1). This exclamation of Eve, the "mother of all the living," is repeated every time a new human being comes into the world. It expresses the woman's joy and awareness that she is sharing in the great mystery of eternal generation.[83]

Jesus said to those who believed in him, "If you continue in my word, you are truly my disciples" (John 8:31). A disciple is someone who hears, accepts, and puts into practice every day the teachings

---

[82] Hemesath, *Slave to Priest*, 36.

[83] John Paul II, Apostolic Letter *Mulieris Dignitatem: On the Dignity and Vocation of Women* (August 15, 1988), no. 18.

of Jesus Christ and the Catholic Church. By our birth into the life of faith through Baptism, we are all called to be disciples. The greatest of all Christ's followers—the Blessed Virgin Mary—serves as the model of true discipleship for us today.

Fr. Tolton's mother, Martha Jane, was an icon of both the physical and spiritual aspects of motherhood perfected in the Blessed Virgin Mary. Martha Jane lived a life rooted in love of God, prayer, and sacrifice beautifully paralleling the life of the Mother of Jesus. The Mother of Priests and the mother of a priest serve as wonderful examples of the indispensable role women play both in God's plan for salvation history and in the experience of families living in a morally corrupt world that needs the witness of authentic disciples. "Be blameless and innocent, children of God without blemish in the midst of a crooked and perverse generation, among whom you shine as lights in the world" (Phil. 2:15).

The biblical foundation for the distinctively feminine contribution to discipleship can be found in the book of Genesis. In Genesis 3, Satan arrives on the scene and begins his attack on the family—which is still his number-one target—seeking to destroy the covenant relationship with God. He enacts his plan by pursuing the woman first. Why her?

"In God's eternal plan, woman is the one in whom the order of love in the created world of persons takes first root. The order of love belongs to the intimate life of God himself, the life of the Trinity. In the intimate life of God, the Holy Spirit is the personal hypostasis of love. Through the Spirit, Uncreated Gift, love becomes a gift for created persons."[84] In other words, in God's mind from all eternity, when He decided to create beings in His image and likeness, and imbue them with life-giving love, it is within a woman's being—within her heart and soul—where His love

[84] Ibid., no. 29.

establishes a foundation and home. By their very nature, all women are mothers (either physical or spiritual); in this way, they share an intimacy with the Holy Spirit as life-bearers and life-givers.

In this sense, women are the ideal examples of what it means to be the teachers of love to all humanity. *"The dignity of woman is measured by the order of love*, which is essentially the order of justice and charity."[85] By targeting the woman, Satan tried to destroy the family by separating the loving and life-giving dimensions of the covenant relationship that flow from the heart of God.

Both men and women are created in the likeness of God but in their distinctiveness, as Pope John Paul II taught, "*women* are more capable than men of paying attention *to another person*, and … the man—even though he shares in the parenting relationship—always remains 'outside' the process of pregnancy and the baby's birth; in many ways he has to *learn* his own '*fatherhood*' from the mother."[86] The woman, in her way of embodying the likeness of God, points to God's immanence since motherhood involves a special communion with the mystery of life as it develops in the womb. In general, a woman's identity is more interiorly focused, intimately linked to her being and "bodiliness" that points to God's "heart"—the intimate exchange of love and life among the Father, Son, and Holy Spirit. The man, in his distinctive way of embodying the image of God, points to God's "otherness" and transcendence; a man's identity, in general, is more exteriorly focused and closely associated with his actions—with the realization of himself in relation to the external world. Their bodies reveal their persons and, within the context of covenant union, tell us something about God's divine identity as the source of all love, intimacy, and communion.

---

[85] Ibid.
[86] Ibid., no. 18.

Fr. Augustus Tolton

There is no greater example of this complementarity-within-unity of man and woman than Joseph and Mary. Mary participated in an intimate, life-giving relationship with God in an interior, bodily way that only a woman could. Joseph was outside of this relationship and had to learn his role as father—as the provider, protector, and servant of the Holy Family—through the Blessed Virgin Mary's motherhood. Mary "is the only productive principle with regard to the human nature of Christ, as much as God the Father is such with regard to the divine nature, and through this she possesses in her virginal motherhood the power of the male fatherhood.... She produces Christ in the flesh through a spiritual power without violation of her virginity, as much as the Father produces Him according to the spirit."[87]

The Tolton family also reflected this unity within their matrimonial and familial relationship. Martha Jane nurtured and gave birth to three children while her husband, in the spirit of St. Joseph, served his family while living on the plantation and sacrificed his life fighting for their freedom. Before her husband's death and long afterward, Mrs. Tolton gave every ounce of her strength to provide for the physical and spiritual welfare of her children. She kept the memory of her husband alive in the hearts and minds of her children, reflecting the sublime truth of the distinctive character of motherhood:

> Although both of them together are parents of their child, *the woman's motherhood constitutes a special "part" in this shared parenthood*, and the most demanding part. Parenthood—even though it belongs to both—is realized much more fully in the woman, especially in the prenatal period. It is the woman

---

[87] Matthias Joseph Scheeben, *Mariology*, vol. 1, 2nd ed. (New York: B. Herder, 1946), 175.

who "pays" directly for this shared generation, which literally absorbs the energies of her body and soul. It is therefore necessary that the man be fully aware that in their shared parenthood he owes a *special debt to the woman.*[88]

In *Behold the Man*, I wrote:

Prior to the Fall, the consciences of the man and his wife were directed toward their Ultimate End: the Beatific Vision, life forever in heaven with God. Satan, through his lies and deceptions, forms the consciences of our first parents away from God and toward themselves. Sadly, the devil has been using the same technique over and over again, century after century and millennium after millennium, that continues to destroy the hearts, minds, and lives of those who seek life-giving communion with God.[89]

After the Fall, God is also able to use human history, even the everyday course of events, to bring about His divine plan. In the Incarnation, where the Eternal Word took flesh in the womb of the Virgin Mary, God the Father says something wonderful: that we are called to draw deeply from the Fountain of Life, that we possess the spark of the Divine within us, and that we have the freedom to abandon ourselves in His love. The Blessed Mother and Martha Jane Tolton show us firsthand through their incredible witness and example of obedience and discipleship how to live in the presence of God.

Despite our sins, the God of love, in His infinite mercy, does not leave us without hope. He intervenes in history, setting in motion a plan for man's redemption: Since it was through the heart

---

[88] John Paul II, *Mulieris Dignitatem* 18.
[89] Burke-Sivers, *Behold the Man*, 28.

of love—the first woman—that sin entered into the world, it will be through that same heart of love—the most blessed of all women—that God effects salvation for the world. The covenant of love and life lost through the no of the "mother of all living" (Gen. 3:20) will be restored in Christ through the yes of the Mother of the Redeemer. This is why families, if they are to overcome the slavery to sin, must foster a deeper affection for and devotion to the Blessed Virgin Mary. Eve offered us fruit born from the tree that led to death; the New Eve brings forth the fruit of her womb, Who gives us everlasting life.

In accepting God's will in faith and love as Mary did at the Incarnation and at the foot of the Cross, Martha Jane Tolton allowed herself to become vulnerable before the Lord, and this vulnerability opened her heart to accept the suffering of a life filled with severe trials: the brutality of slavery, the painful separation from her parents and brother, the deaths of her husband and son, and the agonizing journey toward priesthood for Augustus. In this way, Martha Jane imaged the woman Mary, the Immaculate Heart of love through whom God pours His love into our hearts and who allows us to unite our souls with hers through the suffering we endure.

Our cooperation with the Holy Spirit, who always leads us to Jesus, can be fully realized only in a loving relationship of communion, to which God calls us through suffering. Martha Jane's example of unwavering fidelity shows us that this cooperation happens by grace, and that the only thing that we contribute is our free-willed *fiat* (our yes) in submission to His holy will. The work of salvation belongs to God; nevertheless, we all have a role to play through our cooperation (see Col. 1:24; Phil. 1:29–30). By making ourselves vulnerable before God's holy will through the pierced soul of the Virgin Mary, we can truly unite our hearts and wills to the heart and will of Christ, and make more fully ours what

He has accomplished on the Cross: personal and life-giving union with the Father.

> As we contemplate this Mother, whose heart "a sword has pierced" (cf. Luke 2:35), our thoughts go to *all the suffering women in the world*, suffering either physically or morally. In this suffering a woman's sensitivity plays a role, even though she often succeeds in resisting suffering better than a man.... We may recall her maternal care for her children, especially when they fall sick or fall into bad ways; the death of those most dear to her; the loneliness of mothers forgotten by their grown up children; the loneliness of widows; the sufferings of women who struggle alone to make a living; and women who have been wronged or exploited.... With these sufferings too we must place ourselves at the foot of the Cross.[90]

The Virgin Mary's yes to becoming the Mother of God and Martha Jane Tolton's yes to God's will for her life show not only their complete trust in God and the depth of their discipleship but "a complete openness to the person of Christ, to his whole work, to his whole mission,"[91] which, for mothers, is the complete giving of oneself, body and soul, to the raising of children.

> Motherhood involves a special communion with the mystery of life, as it develops in the woman's womb. The mother is filled with wonder at this mystery of life, and "understands" with unique intuition what is happening inside her. In the light of the "beginning", the mother accepts and loves as a person the child she is carrying in her womb. This unique

---

[90] John Paul II, *Mulieris Dignitatem* 19.
[91] John Paul II, Encyclical Letter *Redemptoris Mater* (*Mother of the Redeemer*) (March 25, 1987), no. 39.

contact with the new human being developing within her gives rise to an attitude towards human beings—not only towards her own child, but every human being—which profoundly marks the woman's personality.[92]

Like any child, Fr. Tolton had some of the physical features and mannerisms of his mother. People probably said, "He has Martha Jane's eyes," or, "He has his mother's smile." What do people say about us as Catholics? We are called, like Martha Jane Tolton, to imitate Christ and to become courageous disciples every day. Can people see the face of Jesus in us? Can people say to us, "You have the heart of Jesus," or, "I can see the light of Christ burning within you"? Our Baptism and Confirmation leaves the permanent mark of God imprinted on our souls, and like Mary, who bore God in her womb, we bear God within us each time we receive the Blessed Sacrament. How do we give birth to God's love and truth through this great gift of His love? How well do we bear the labor pains of ridicule from a society that mocks us because of our Catholic Faith? How do we give life and meaning to our Faith amid a culture of sin and death? Mary and Martha Jane show us the way. The mothers of Jesus and Augustus not only gave life to their sons through their bodies, but their fruitfulness continued through their example of quiet prayerfulness, deep humility, patient obedience, steadfast hope, and enduring love. We can and must make these women's virtues our own if we are to become true disciples and the people God created us to be.

The triumph of God's love through Mary's Immaculate Heart frees us for participation in works of mercy, thereby bringing God's light into the world. "Jesus spoke to them saying, 'I am the light of

[92] John Paul II, *Mulieris Dignitatem* 18.

the world; he who follows me will not walk in darkness, but will have the light of life'" (John 8:12). The Virgin Mary serves as the epitome of discipleship and obedience to God's will, allowing herself to be used as an instrument for God's glory.

The life of the Tolton family, epitomized by its matriarch, exemplifies God's loving condescension in becoming flesh and dwelling among us (John 1:14). Jesus understands what it is like to live in the depths of poverty. He understands what it is like to experience great sadness and humiliation, unbelievable pain and suffering, and even the darkness of death itself. God wants us to know that we are not alone. In Martha Jane Tolton, the Lord gives us a woman who humbled herself in love before God and opened her heart to His holy will, devoting herself completely to discipleship in Christ. Therefore, through Mary's perfect example of what it means to be fully human and being inspired by Martha Jane's indomitable faith, we too can share in the divine life of the Trinity and participate in God's saving plan for the destiny of all mankind.

> Motherhood has been introduced into the order of the Covenant that God made with humanity in Jesus Christ. Each and every time that *motherhood* is repeated in human history, it is always *related to the Covenant* which God established with the human race through the motherhood of the Mother of God.... The *motherhood* of every woman, understood in the light of the Gospel, is similarly not only "of flesh and blood": it expresses a profound "*listening to the word of the living God*" and a readiness to "safeguard" this Word, which is "the word of eternal life" (cf. John 6:68). For it is precisely those born of earthly mothers, the sons and daughters of the human race, who receive from the Son of God the power to become "children of God" (John 1:12).... The history

of every human being passes through the threshold of a woman's motherhood.[93]

Every time we hear the Word of God at Mass and receive the Eucharist we become, in a sense, pregnant with the Word Made Flesh and then give birth to Him through evangelization. Christ becomes known and present through us. How do people see Jesus in us? These extraordinary women show us that we must all become receptive wombs for God's Word so that, filled with the Holy Spirit and nurtured by the grace of the sacraments, we will give life to Christ by bearing witness to God's love and truth in the world through our Catholic Faith.

Mary and Martha Jane point the way to Jesus. Through their beautiful example of motherhood, fidelity, and sanctity, humanity inherits the gift of living signposts along the road to salvation. Though they rose to extraordinary holiness, it is in the simple day-to-day events of home life that these women of God shine forth as models of noble simplicity and grace-filled charity in their families. Their common mission and greatest desire is for us to find Jesus and bring Him fully into our hearts and homes.

Fr. Augustus Tolton died fourteen years before his mother. In a life already filled with tremendous suffering, Martha Jane Tolton had to bear the cross of every parent's greatest fear. All of us who have children believe and expect that they will outlive us, but Martha Jane had to bear the loss of her son (and second child) at forty-three years old, just as the Blessed Virgin Mary had to endure her only Son's Passion and Death at the age of thirty-three.

What might Fr. Tolton have said at his mother's funeral Mass, had he lived to celebrate it? I have had the sad honor of eulogizing my mother—like Martha Jane, a strong black woman who raised

---

[93] Ibid., no. 19.

a black son who strives for faithfulness. The following attempt to construct what Fr. Tolton might have said is based on those remarks:

> When I think of my mother's life, I cannot help but draw parallels to the life of Christ. Our Lord was born humble and poor in a stable. My mother, Martha Jane, was born poor and a slave on the Manning family plantation.
>
> Our Lord left His country of origin and lived for a number of years in Egypt. My mother, who lived in Kentucky, was given away as a wedding dowry and taken against her will from her family to Missouri. She would later escape with her three children through the Underground Railroad to Illinois.
>
> Jesus was a carpenter by profession, and my mother did the very best she could to create a warm, loving home for my father and siblings in our tiny, one-room slave cabin.
>
> Jesus was a healer who worked many miracles. The night we escaped from slavery and in the days that followed—led by my mother holding my sister in her arms while my brother and I carried a small supply of food—we barely evaded arrest by Confederate soldiers and were nearly shot as Mom struggled to maneuver a rowboat across the Mississippi River. It is truly a miracle that we survived.
>
> But the most significant ways in which my mother's life paralleled the life of Christ were in her sacrifice and suffering. The needs of my father and her children always came first. When we arrived in Quincy, she worked long hours—ten hours or more per day, six days a week—in a tobacco factory filled with the nauseating smell of nicotine. Mom's heart was broken when my older brother, Charley, died of pneumonia when he was only ten years old. She

shielded us as best she could from the stinging racial slurs and belittling epithets of parishioners who mistreated our family because of our skin color. My mother worked side by side with me in the lay apostolate, evangelizing fallen-away Catholics and catechizing children. During the long, agonizing struggle to become a priest, my mother's prayers, support, and encouragement strengthened me. She would say to me constantly, "Never forget the goodness of the Lord."

My mother knew that her suffering, especially during the last years of her life, had a special place in God's saving plan. It was, in fact, a sharing in Christ's Passion and a union with the redeeming sacrifice that He offered in obedience to the Father's will. She knew that we exist not to avoid suffering, but to find meaning in the suffering that is unavoidable.

Christ assured his friend Martha, "Your brother Lazarus will rise." This is true because God loves us. His love is so great, so powerful, and so real that He created each and every one of us so that we could participate in and experience that love. It is God's love that brought my mom and each of us out of nothingness and into this world. He loves us, and so we exist!

But now that Martha Jane has died. What happened? Did God stop loving her? Not by a long shot! God's love brought Martha Jane into being, and His love is eternal: It has no end! And because God still loves her, she will live! The love that brought her out of nothingness will bring her back from the dead because we don't worship a dead man: God's love is greater and more powerful than death itself. That is why there is a resurrection on the last day, and that is why we can take strength from God's love today! God will bring us to Heaven when we die, but only if we take hold of Heaven while we live! That is the whole reason we are here: to make the love of Christ come alive by making Jesus the heart of our lives. This is what my mother understood so well.

My brothers and sisters in Christ, Our Lord says, "If any man would come after me, let him deny himself and take up his cross and follow me. For whoever would save his life will lose it; and whoever loses his life for my sake and the gospel's will save it." My mother indeed picked up her cross and followed Christ to glory. When the cross became heavy, she bore its weight with dignity. When her steps slowed to a crawl, she placed her hope in Him who casts out all doubt and fear. When she was racked with pain, she trusted in the Divine Physician, who brought her a healing that this world could not give. And through it all, she had tremendous faith and courage! We now pray for Martha Jane, that this faith will lead her to the full glory of Heaven. When Christ raised Lazarus from the grave, he called Lazarus by name. Because Martha Jane called on the Lord's name, Christ, in His immense love, will say, "Martha Jane, come to life! I did not create you for the grave, but for myself. You have accepted me by faith while on earth. Come, now, and share my life — forever."

The Role of Children

There is no question that the influences of secular thought and culture have a profound influence within and upon our children today. Many of our teenagers and young adults are struggling to hold on to the Catholic belief in absolute truth and, because they have a weak foundation in the Faith, are unable to see how their Faith is connected to their life experience. Instead, our youth align themselves with a society that places itself and not Jesus Christ as the center of all reality and truth.

The formation of children within the family, primarily through their parents' example, must occur and operate within a context of faith and community so that children are continually molded into the image of Christ for the purpose of salvation and evangelization.

To this end, families must nurture an atmosphere of inclusion in all aspects of family and parish life so that youth and young adults "who by Baptism are incorporated into Christ and integrated into the People of God, are made sharers in their particular way in the priestly, prophetic, and kingly office of Christ, and have their own part to play in the mission of the whole Christian people in the Church and in the world."[94] It is within the family — with the support of the parish — that youth should participate in evangelization and faith-sharing activities in order to become living witnesses of God's truth.

All of this must be fostered in the home — the domestic Church and foundation of the parish community — where education in the fundamental truths of the Faith and virtuous living are nurtured through family prayer, including the Rosary, meal prayers, and the breaking open of God's Word in the Scriptures. Martha Jane Tolton understood well that the family's primary duty is spiritual. Her son's income helped the family to make ends meet, but when he had to reduce his hours to pursue theological studies with a Franciscan priest, his mother "told the priest and her son that ... she did not want to put anything in the way of a vocation to the priesthood."[95]

Mothers and fathers should also teach their children that they have a duty, as members of God's family, to all who are in need of

---

[94] CCC 897, quoting *Lumen Gentium* 31.
[95] Hemesath, *Slave to Priest*, 57.

assistance, especially the poor. In this way, children play a vital role in "teaching all people that they have an incomparable dignity."[96] The values taught and affirmed in families should be affirmed and incorporated into society, and society should respect the rights of the family. Youth and young adults, as the hands and feet of Christ, should be fully engaged in the corporal and spiritual works of mercy, in the renewal of the social order in the spirit of the gospel, and in outreach to their peers who are broken and confused about the purpose and meaning of their lives. The witness of Peter Paul and Martha Jane Tolton fueled in the heart of Augustus a deep passion and zeal for serving the poor. "Day after day he was seen coming in and out of the shacks, the rat-infested hovels and tenement houses. He listened compassionately to complaints of unemployment, desertion, injustice, depravity. Fr. Tolton knew how to bring hope and comfort to the sick and dying."[97]

The sacramental dimension of family life must also be encouraged in young people. The home must embody a spirituality that enhances and promotes devotion and active participation in the Eucharist, where "grace is channeled into us and ... the glorification of God, to which all other activities of the Church are directed as toward their goal, are most powerfully achieved."[98] This must be accompanied by a deeper appreciation and understanding of the reality of sin and the need to find healing in God's merciful love through the sacrament of Reconciliation.

---

[96] Richard M. Hogan and John M. LeVoir, *Covenant of Love: Pope John Paul II on Sexuality, Marriage, and the Family in the Modern World*, 2nd ed. (San Francisco: Ignatius Press, 1992), 268.

[97] Hemesath, *Slave to Priest*, 212.

[98] Vatican Council II, Constitution on the Sacred Liturgy *Sacrosanctum Concilium* (December 4, 1963), no. 10, in Walter M. Abbott, S.J., ed., *The Documents of Vatican II* (New York: Corpus Books, 1966).

Fr. Augustus Tolton

Children are special witnesses to God's loving plan in the world and for future generations of Catholic men and women. The mission of the family to evangelize—particularly of parents who are educating their children in the Faith—should "always remain in union with the evangelizing activities of the universal Church."[99] In this way, children will learn how important it is always to remain faithful to the Church's teaching as they work with their parents and their parish community to become "shining witnesses and models of holiness" that reflect the reality and awesome power of God's love in the world.[100] Augustus Tolton served as an example of this: "The regular tutoring by dedicated priests and nuns, his habitual self-discipline, his faithful observance of religious duties, and his twelve years of honest service as a wage earner had formed a character distinguished by determination, integrity, and leadership [that] commanded love and respect from those around him, no matter what shade of color their skins might be."[101]

> It is, above all, the Church as Mother that gives birth to, educates and builds up the Christian family, by putting into effect in its regard the saving mission which she has received from her Lord. By proclaiming the word of God [evangelization], the Church reveals to the Christian family its true identity, what it is and should be according to the Lord's plan; by celebrating the sacraments, the Church enriches and strengthens the Christian family with the grace of Christ for its sanctification to the glory of the Father; by the continuous proclamation of the new commandment

---

[99] Hogan and LeVoir, *Covenant of Love*, 273.
[100] Vatican Council II, Dogmatic Constitution on the Church *Lumen Gentium* (November 21, 1964), no. 39, in Walter M. Abbott, S.J., ed., *The Documents of Vatican II* (New York: Corpus Books, 1966).
[101] Hemesath, *Slave to Priest*, 113.

of love, the Church encourages and guides the Christian family to the service of love, so that it may imitate and relive the same self-giving and sacrificial love that the Lord Jesus has for the entire human race.... In this way, while the Christian family is a fruit and sign of the supernatural fecundity of the Church, it stands also as a symbol, witness and participant of the Church's motherhood.[102]

Children today are thirsty, and the Lord invites them to come and drink from the never-ending wellspring of His grace and love. God wants their hearts, so that, in His love, they may be transformed. Our children do not walk alone on this path to holiness: The Virgin Mary and Our Lord Jesus Christ are with them, encouraging them to place all of their trust in God alone, freely, willingly, and lovingly. When parents empower their children to say yes in response to the grace they have received in Baptism, they will find true happiness and peace — a peace that can come only from a total gift of self to our heavenly Father. Fr. Tolton would often spend hours in prayer, reveling in the knowledge that "comfort and consolation came to him from the Divine Presence. He knew that God understood him, guided him, and directed him."[103]

This requires, of course, reciprocity from children in the form of respect and obedience:

Finally, as long as a child lives at home with his parents, the child should obey his parents in all that they ask of him when it is for his good or that of the family. "Children, obey your parents in everything, for this pleases the Lord" (Col.

---

[102] John Paul II, Apostolic Exhortation *Familiaris Consortio: On the Role of the Christian Family in the Modern World* (November 22, 1981), no. 49.

[103] Hemesath, *Slave to Priest*, 216.

3:20; cf. Eph. 6:1). Children should also obey the reasonable directions of their teachers and all to whom their parents have entrusted them.... As they grow up, children should continue to respect their parents. They should anticipate their wishes, willingly seek their advice, and accept their just admonitions. Obedience toward parents ceases with the emancipation of the children; not so respect, which is always owed to them. This respect has its roots in the fear of God, one of the gifts of the Holy Spirit.[104]

This was also true for Our Lord. Consider what occurred when Mary and Joseph found Him in the temple when He was twelve years old:

And when they saw him they were astonished; and his mother said to him, "Son, why have you treated us so? Behold, your father and I have been looking for you anxiously." And he said to them, "How is it that you sought me? Did you not know that I must be in my Father's house?" And they did not understand the saying that he spoke to them. And he went down with them and came to Nazareth, and was obedient to them; and his mother kept all these things in her heart. And Jesus increased in wisdom and in stature, and in favor with God and man. (Luke 2:41–52)

If children are truly to be followers of Christ, they must follow His example of obedience in faith. They must die to their own wills, which keep them from becoming who God intended them to be in Christ Jesus. They must learn to open their hearts to the Holy Spirit so that, like Christ, they may not follow their own will or the opinions of the world, but actively pursue and embrace the

[104] CCC 2217.

will of our Father in Heaven.[105] "I take delight in your promise like one who finds a treasure.... The lovers of your law have great peace; they never stumble.... My soul obeys your will and loves it dearly. I obey your precepts and your will; all that I do is before you" (Ps. 119:162, 165, 167–168).

Our young people should remember these two things: As parents, we will not always tell them what they want to hear, but if they listen to us with their hearts and with the grace of the Holy Spirit, our advice may eventually lead them toward their ultimate happiness and fulfillment: a deep, personal, loving relationship with Jesus Christ — something that drugs, alcohol, sex, and even their friends cannot begin to offer them. "For Fr. Tolton there were no lonely hours in the rectory, because his devoted mother, whom he cherished above all others, was always there to help, comfort, and encourage."[106]

Second, we parents may not be as "in the know" or as "cool" as our children think we are; we may not always understand their music and choice of clothes, but they should know this: We would rather die than see them participate in self-destructive behavior. We love them more than they will ever know, but our love for them does not even come close to the love that God has for them, which is as if they were the only person who has ever existed. Our greatest hope for our children flows from our greatest gift to them: our teaching them — by our example — what it means to be fully alive in their Catholic Faith.

A Biblical Parallel: The Holy Family

I'm not sure which reaction bothers me the most when people hear that my wife and I have four children: the "Oh my goodness"

---

[105] CCC 606; John 6:38.
[106] Hemesath, *Slave to Priest*, 216.

gasp of unbelief as if I just told them I was dying of cancer; or the wide-eyed grimace of "Wow, I am truly sorry for you two; I'm glad that's not me"; or the belittling laughter of "You guys are insane; there's no way I'm having that many kids." Just once I would like to hear someone say, "I am so glad to see that there are husbands and wives who love children more than luxury vacations and expensive cars." Just once it would be nice to hear, "I am so pleased to see in this day and age that there are married couples who are open to the gift of life that God has graciously allowed us to share in."

We live in a culture where children are viewed and treated like diseases that need to be eliminated. If you think this is an exaggeration, consider the views of Princeton University professor Peter Singer, whom the *New Yorker* has called the "most influential" philosopher alive.[107] He was asked the question, "What about parents conceiving and giving birth to a child specifically to kill him, take his organs and transplant them into their ill older children?" Professor Singer replied, "They're not doing something really wrong in itself."[108] The follow-up question asked, "Is anything wrong with a society in which children are bred for spare parts on a massive scale?" Professor Singer replied, "No."[109]

Over lunch, the interviewer read back Dr. Singer's answers to him. Not only did he stand by his statements, but he added that it would be ethically acceptable to kill one-year-old children with physical or mental disabilities—though ideally the question of killing these children would have been raised as soon as possible

---

[107] Marvin Olasky, "The Most Influential Philosopher Alive," Townhall.com, December 2, 2004, https://townhall.com/columnists/marvinolasky/2004/12/02/the-most-influential-philosopher-alive-n984666.

[108] Ibid.

[109] Ibid.

after birth.[110] All this came from a man who, according to the *New England Journal of Medicine*, has had more success in effecting changes in acceptable behavior than any philosopher in the last century.[111]

The effects of all this on our children unfold every day before our eyes. Our schools form our children in political correctness and values-neutral education that promote ideas that, left unchecked, will destroy their faith. All this is done in the name of "tolerance" and "diversity," but it is at the expense of authentic truth and freedom. These ideas will lead them to embrace a secular Christ without the Cross.

I don't know how Joseph and Mary did it. I sometimes try to imagine what it must have been like to trust in and be fully dependent upon God's divine providence continually. Mary and Joseph possessed immense courage and enduring faith at a time of tremendous upheaval early in their marriage. Their lives were turned completely upside down, and yet Mary and Joseph lovingly followed God's will for them, even without understanding the still-unfolding mystery of His plan in salvation history—and the pivotal role they played in it.

Sometimes we have to look back before we can move forward. Doing so, we can see that the family has its origin in that love with which the Creator embraces each of us. This family relationship is so central to God's plan for us that He chose to be born and grow up in a family, entering into human history with a mother and father. In a culture in which privilege, wealth, and prestige mean everything, our Father in Heaven shows us in the simple lives of a housewife and a carpenter that "the divine mystery of the Incarnation of the Word has an intimate connection with the human

---

[110] Ibid.
[111] Ibid.

family."[112] Through the family, God unites Himself in a special way to each of us, for God Himself "labored with human hands and loved with a human heart."[113] The family is where Jesus learned the love and respect that children must have for their parents, which was the first expression of His obedience to the will of the Father—and which would ultimately lead to our salvation.[114]

The author Rick Sarkisian, in his work on the role of the family in guiding us to Heaven, reflects on this special connection:

> The Holy Family offers us rich insight into God's view of the family [and is] a model of family life full of beauty, truth, and goodness. The Holy Family was united with Heaven at the birth of Jesus, and shared in the normal, day-to-day activities common to families of that time. There were struggles, to be sure, yet this family ate, talked, prayed, worked, laughed, traveled, and grew together. They were [living witnesses] of God's plan for family togetherness.[115]

"The Christian family is a communion of persons, a sign and image of the communion of the Father and the Son in the Holy Spirit [that] is called to [participate in] the prayer and sacrifice of Christ."[116] For the Holy Family, Sarkisian continues, "God was at the center of their home and at the center of their individual lives. Obedience and humility were particularly evident, such as Mary and Joseph's acceptance of God's plan to be parents of the Messiah and their continuing surrender to God's will after the birth of Jesus. Joseph and Mary were Holy Spouses united in common

---

[112] John Paul II, *Letter to Families* 2.
[113] Ibid.
[114] Ibid.
[115] Rick Sarkisian, Ph.D., *The Mission of the Catholic Family: On the Pathway to Heaven* (San Diego: Basilica Press, 1999), 5–6.
[116] CCC 2205.

faith and acceptance of God's will, regardless of the circumstances or outcome."[117]

The Fourth Commandment tells us to honor our father and mother. This means that children are to show respect and gratitude to their parents, who have brought them into the world and enabled them to grow in stature, wisdom, and grace.[118] This respect is shown primarily through obedience — not the blind obedience of a mindless robot or a trained pet, but the obedience of faith: a spirit in which children, with humility and generosity, revere and continually strive to fulfill the will of God with the loving guidance of their parents.

"On the family's journey to the Father, we must not overlook the importance of [the Holy Family] as timeless teachers for our role as parents. Joseph [and Mary] taught Jesus important lessons about life, as we must do with our children."[119] Fathers and mothers must teach their children about the meaning of authentic manhood and womanhood rooted in our Christian faith. "If we do not get involved with our children's voyage to adulthood, then, by default, the world gets involved. All kinds of distorted images follow, dumped on our kids by TV, movies, magazines, sports, and other media figures that pitch superficial images [in an] attempt to shape who they should be as men and women. Instead, our example should be the Holy Family, who offers all of us a path to holiness, and through whom we enter the core of the salvation message."[120]

We must do whatever it takes to prepare our children for Heaven. Mothers and fathers must accept the responsibility that comes with raising children and not delegate their obligations to

---

[117] Sarkisian, *Mission of the Catholic Family*, 6.
[118] See CCC 2215.
[119] Sarkisian, *Mission of the Catholic Family*, 9.
[120] Ibid.

catechists, teachers, or coaches. Children's primary role models and examples for living their Christian faith should be their parents, whom God sets in honor and authority over them (see Sir. 3:2). St. Paul reminds us that this authority is to be exercised with heartfelt compassion, kindness, humility, gentleness, patience, and, above all, love, which is the bond of perfection that unites us to Jesus and draws us ever deeper into the heart of our heavenly Father (see Col. 3:12, 14).

Chapter 4

The Power of Prayer

Prayer as an Act of Faith and Trust

A generation after the death of Fr. Tolton, Mother Teresa, when she was still a young nun, felt called to serve God in a special way. In a letter to the archbishop of Calcutta, she wrote:

> I have been and am very happy as a Loreto nun. To leave that which I love and expose myself to new labors and sufferings which will be great, to be the laughing stock of so many, to cling to and choose deliberately the hard things of life, to loneliness and disgrace, to uncertainty—and all because Jesus wants it; because something is calling me to leave all to live His life and to do His work.[121]

Mother Teresa is speaking to us about making a complete gift of ourselves, where the seeds of prayer are nourished in the rich soil of loving obedience to God's will. When we entered into an intimate relationship and life-giving communion with God in our Baptism, each of us was personally called to do His will. But at times our prayer life is hindered by sin, and we feel very distant from God and unworthy to fulfill what He has planned for us. It

---

[121] Jim Gallagher, *Mother Teresa: Road to Sainthood* (London: Catholic Truth Society, 2003), 31.

is only after the obstacle of sin is removed and we are filled with the Holy Spirit that we are able to see the road clearly in front of us, and are empowered with the confidence to move forward with assurance and joy: "Here am I! Send me" (Isa. 6:8).

To respond faithfully to God's voice, we must trust God enough to come before Him in humility and love, and not be afraid to expose the deepest parts of who we are so that His mercy can shine forth in and through the unique person He created us to be. It means saying with Christ, "I have come ... not to do my own will, but the will of him who sent me" (John 6:38).

Our yes to God's holy will provides the road map for a life of prayer. Even when we forget about God for a while, He tirelessly calls each person to that mysterious encounter known as prayer. In prayer, God's initiative of love always comes first; our own first step is always a response. As God gradually reveals Himself and as He makes a complete gift of Himself to us in love, "prayer becomes a reciprocal call,"[122] an acceptance of God's invitation to a covenant relationship—intimate, personal, loving, and life-giving communion.

We are looking for relationship with God, and we are not whole until we are in God. The apostle John reminds us that "God is love, and he who abides in love abides in God, and God abides in him" (1 John 4:16). The way we get "in God" is through prayer, which allows us to enter into communion with Him as we make our way to Heaven. We pray because we love. We pray because we want to deepen and strengthen our relationship with God. We pray because we want to give ourselves over totally to God. We pray because prayer moves us from knowing *about* God to knowing God. This is why, like Jesus, we must enter into the wilderness; we must enter

---

[122] CCC 2567.

into that place of letting go. In the wilderness, we seek God's face as we share in the very suffering of Jesus Christ and experience the power of His Resurrection.

The Mystery of Christ's Passion, Death, and Resurrection always calls us to a new life. This new life requires us to let go of the old, just as faith requires that we surrender everything to God. Letting go is never easy. We must look to Jesus as our example of what it means to make a gift of our lives, because it is in giving ourselves away that we truly find ourselves. When we pray, we ask God to lower the walls that we have erected between Him and ourselves so that, by the power of the Holy Spirit, Jesus can enter into our most guarded places and set us free to love. Christ allows us to see and understand that by the power of God, and none other, we can be transformed by prayer. We must take our hands off the steering wheel and let God drive. We must empty ourselves of sin so that God can fill us with His love. We must die to the ways of this world so that Christ can live in us. "I appeal to you therefore, brethren, by the mercies of God, to present your bodies as a living sacrifice, holy and acceptable to God, which is your spiritual worship. Do not be conformed to this world but be transformed by the renewal of your mind, that you may prove what is the will of God, what is good and acceptable and perfect" (Rom. 12:1–2).

Prayer is both a gift of grace and a response that takes effort on our part. In order for us to walk humbly before our God in the obedience of faith, we must appreciate the fact that we need God's help every step of the way, especially during those times when we feel as if God is not hearing or answering our prayers.

A number of years ago, my best friend since childhood—who stood next to me when I married my wife—died of cancer at thirty-eight. He left behind a wife and two small children. The five groomsmen at his wedding were pallbearers at his funeral.

Fr. Augustus Tolton

There was so much sadness that weekend. I will never forget the image of my friend's stoic mother alongside his anguished wife when the casket was closed for the last time. It was one of the most difficult and painful experiences of my life. I kept thinking, "How are they going to get past this? How is his wife going to manage a full-time career while raising her sons alone? How do you give praise and thanks to God—how do you even trust God—at a time like this?"

The experience of prayerful trust in the midst of severe trials was very familiar to Augustus Tolton. He had hoped and prayed for years to become a priest but was met with one heartbreaking rejection after another. "His faith was repeatedly subjected to the severest test.... Days and weeks of disillusionment and frustration at times drove him to the brink of madness. But it was also an opportunity for gaining moral strength and courage.... 'The unmistakable will of God', he moaned in times of extreme desolation."[123]

"Faith is the theological virtue by which we believe in God and believe all that he has said and revealed to us, and that Holy Mother Church proposes for our belief, because Christ is truth itself."[124] Faith allows us to see God's loving presence in all of the events in our lives. Whether we are in a fortunate or difficult situation, with faith we can discover God's providence in it. Anyone who truly believes in God and His infinite love gives himself over to Him totally. And in that complete self-giving, he finds the peace and certainty for which his heart longs. This was the invariable hope of Martha Jane Tolton, who, whether in times of intense joy or sorrow, would continually utter a simple yet powerful prayer that became the lens through which her life was focused: "Never forget the goodness of the Lord."[125]

---

[123] Hemesath, *Slave to Priest*, 122.
[124] CCC 1814.
[125] Hemesath, *Slave to Priest*, 123.

How does prayer help build a strong faith? Prayer is speaking heart-to-heart with God in a relationship of love and trust. Therefore, trust is one of the ways we put our faith into action. And the biggest inhibitor of trust is fear. We fear that God may not answer our prayer in the way we desire or expect. We are afraid to step out in faith when God calls us to trust Him. We are afraid of becoming uncomfortable when God invites us to take our relationship with Him to the next level. The antidote to fear is love: "There is no fear in love, but perfect love casts out fear.... He who fears is not perfected in love" (1 John 4:18).

Jesus prayed before He went to the Cross, and it is precisely these dry, dark periods in our lives—when we are faced with the reality of praying from a place of disillusion and anxiety—that lead us into the very heart of Christ's Paschal Mystery. The real "cross" of prayer is to believe that Jesus Christ is Lord of every single situation in our lives—that is, to trust in God's merciful love through prayer even when we are experiencing great difficulties. During these times, prayer feels like a heavy burden instead of an act of love, but therein lies the mystery: The cross is the definitive sign of sacrificial love.

Nothing can separate us from the love of God, and how we respond to the Lord's activity in our lives reflects our trust in His love for us. If we want prayer to become not simply *what we do* but *who we are*, we must wait on God and have complete confidence in His mercy and love.

Year after year, like the changing of the seasons, the Tolton family embraced the seemingly endless cycle of fervent prayer and unwavering trust with patient hope that God would respond to their petitions and open the door to priesthood for Augustus. "For hours, sometimes far into the night, mother and son talked about it and waited and planned and prayed."[126]

---

[126] Ibid., 118.

Fr. Augustus Tolton

Not long ago, in the church parking lot during Mass, someone broke into our minivan. Since then, I have often wondered what my reaction would be if I ever came face-to-face with the individual who committed this crime against my family. What would I say to the person who frightened my children, who demolished my family's sense of security, who made me feel helpless? I know what I would want to do, but, as a follower of Jesus, the more important question is: "What does Christ call me to do?"

But what happened to my family pales in comparison with the suffering others have had to endure. In the midst of unimaginable anguish and pain, Jesus calls us to do the seemingly impossible: He tells us that we must forgive. Our Lord gives us no other options and makes no exceptions. This was a hard lesson in discipleship that Fr. Tolton had to learn. In a particularly emotional exchange during a private tutoring session with one of his mentors, Fr. Michael Richardt, the young Augustus Tolton lamented that

> Negroes … died of inhuman treatment, hard labor, or starvation. Everyone knows that black slaves were put to death because of old age or incurable disease, that crippled or sickly infants were killed outright.… The laws against murder were never enforced in cases dealing with Negroes. Many white people in the South—and elsewhere too—treated the slaves like animals. In fact, the Negroes were accounted even lower than the beasts.… I am thinking of the thousands, in fact, millions of slaves … who lived in America after they were kidnapped from Africa or sold at auction. All this came to mind when I studied St. Thomas' definition of justice. Generation after generation of white people not only deprived Negro slaves of mental and moral development, but they squelched their natural potential by shackling them to intolerable labor, flogging them mercilessly, and subjecting them

to inhuman cruelties.... Why are we too often given the lowest jobs, the poorest pay, the worst homes, and the most unsanitary living conditions? Why can't we go to Catholic schools and churches without being insulted? Why do some people despise us, hate us, call us niggers, bastards, coons? Why are we isolated like lepers, segregated, shoved aside, kicked, spit upon?[127]

Fr. Richardt taught the future priest that the cross of Christ is the meaning of love and the cornerstone of forgiveness and mercy: "The Church always stands for right and justice. Members of the Church, however, since they are human beings, often fall short of the ideals of Christ and his Church.... Let us face the situation like men — like Christians; let us do our part to spread the kingdom of God on earth."[128]

Forgiveness was so essential to the purpose and mission of Christ that when the apostles asked Jesus how to pray, he gave them the Our Father, in which we ask God to "forgive us our trespasses as we forgive those who trespass against us." Christ wanted to make a very strong and direct link between God's forgiving us and our forgiving others.

God wanted to show us, once and for all, that despite our sin, He loves us and wants to save us. "By embracing in His human heart the Father's love for men," Jesus showed us that when we freely choose to do the Father's will — when we freely choose what is good, true, and beautiful — even suffering and death cannot overpower God's love for us.[129] God literally loves us to death. He sent His only Son to die in order to show us that when we freely give up that which is most precious to us, our very lives, in order to do

[127] Ibid., 106–109.
[128] Ibid., 111–112.
[129] CCC 609.

the Father's will, God will give us everlasting life. The life of Fr. Augustus Tolton is a testimony to the fact that even in our darkest hour, God's love knows no end; that in the hardships of everyday life, God's love knows no bounds; that in our suffering and death, God's love holds nothing back.

Conversion is the key to building a "perfect" love—that is, a mature and complete relationship of love and trust with God. For the apostles, *metanoia* (a Greek word meaning "turning one's mind around") meant a complete separation from their previous lives: "Immediately they left their nets and followed him" (Mark 1:18). They put their total trust in Jesus, leaving behind their only means of livelihood, not knowing where it would all lead.

Fr. Tolton's *metanoia* experience came when he was sixteen years old, on the day of his first Holy Communion. "Augustine remembered that his heart leaped with a strange exhilaration when Fr. McGirr told the meaning of the words: 'Do this in commemoration of me.' ... He imagined himself at the altar offering Mass and speaking before the congregation about the 'goodness of the Lord.'"[130] Like Fr. Augustus, we are called by God to step out in faith and trust. "The prayer of faith consists not only in saying, 'Lord, Lord,' but in disposing our hearts to do the will of the Father. Jesus calls his disciples to bring into their prayer this concern for cooperating with the divine plan,"[131] summarized in the definitive prayer of Christ, where we say with confidence, "Thy will be done."

But Satan is hard at work! We live in a culture that finds it easier to believe a lie than to live the truth and that embraces the thirty-second sound bite as if it were divine revelation, crowding out the responsibilities of faith lived in the light of truth, goodness, and beauty.

[130] Hemesath, *Slave to Priest*, 54–55.
[131] CCC 2611.

God calls us to exercise spiritual boldness!

In Christ, and through his human will, the will of the Father has been perfectly fulfilled once for all. Jesus said on entering into this world: "Lo, I have come to do your will, O God" (Heb. 10:7; Ps. 40:7).... In the prayer of his agony, he consents totally to this will: "not my will, but Thine be done" (Luke 22:42; cf. John 4:34; 5:30; 6:38). For this reason Jesus "gave himself for our sins to deliver us from the present evil age, according to the will of our God and Father" (Gal. 1:4).[132]

I often think of what was running through St. Paul's mind during the three days he was blind after meeting Jesus and before his baptism. In the silence of his heart, as he tried to grasp the meaning of repentance and conversion, I imagine him saying (borrowing words from Thomas Merton):

My Lord God, I have no idea where I am going. I do not see the road ahead of me. I cannot know for certain where it will end. Nor do I really know myself and the fact that I think that I am following your will does not mean that I am actually doing so. But I believe that the desire to please you does in fact please you. And I hope I have that desire in all that I am doing. I hope that I will never do anything apart from that desire. And I know that if I do this, you will lead me by the right road though I may know nothing about it. Therefore, I will trust you always though I may seem to be lost and in the shadow of death. I will not fear, for you are ever with me, and you will never leave me to face my perils alone.[133]

---

[132] CCC 2824.

[133] Thomas Merton, *Thoughts in Solitude* (New York: Farrar, Straus and Giroux, 1999), 79.

Fr. Augustus Tolton

The Scriptures proclaim, "The Lord is my light and my help; whom shall I fear? The Lord is the stronghold of my life; before whom shall I shrink?... Hope in him, hold firm and take heart. Trust in the Lord!" (Ps. 27:1, 14). Jesus Christ revealed to Paul, to Fr. Tolton, and to us that He is the beacon of hope that illumines our path through the turbulent sea of life.

Through the extraordinary life of America's first black priest, Jesus speaks powerfully to us who peer into the darkness of our morally corrupt culture and ask, "Is there anything at all that makes sense?" Jesus answers this question and, in fact, sums up the entire Christian message in one sentence when He proclaims that God so loved the world that He gave his only-begotten Son that the world might believe and have eternal life (see John 3:16). The only thing that makes sense is God's total, perfect, and unconditional love, through which He gives us His Son to be the Light of the world. God "is nothing but love — love that goes as far as the Father sacrificing his Son out of love for the world. There is nothing more for him to give us." All that remains is our choice to either "accept God's love so that it can prove effective and fruitful in us, or cower in our darkness in order to evade the light of this love."[134]

The call of the Lord is going out to each one of us. Are we ready to answer? Are we ready to follow? Is anxiety, pride, or an unwillingness to detach ourselves from the things of this world keeping us from the total freedom that radical conversion brings? I asked myself this very question while discerning God's call to leave my career in campus law enforcement and dedicate the rest of my life to serving the Church on a full-time basis in my apostolate. Even though I knew God was calling me, I was afraid to "let go" and have complete trust in His will. I looked to close friends, my wife, and Fr. Tolton

---

[134] Hans Urs von Balthasar, *Light of the Word: Brief Reflections on the Sunday Readings* (San Francisco: Ignatius Press, 1993), 178.

for inspiration and guidance, and found the courage to leave what was safe and comfortable to follow Jesus unconditionally, without looking back. Our Lord says, "No one who puts his hand to the plow and looks back is fit for the kingdom of God" (Luke 9:62). *Metanoia* is never easy, but the experience of joy and peace that Christ has given to me and my family far exceeded my expectations and imagination. *Now* is the time to put our lives in order, to reexamine our priorities, and to put Christ first in our lives above and before all else.

The key is never to stop praying; never to stop learning about the Faith; never to stop asking questions; never to stop struggling; and to live the Faith that we profess with great joy and enthusiasm! We must make a connection between the Faith that we learn and the lived experience of that Faith. Sometimes this means picking up our cross and following Christ with the understanding that living the truth — that being the people God created us to be — means being countercultural. Christ did not die so that His teachings could be changed by the culture: Christ died so that His love and His truth could change the world!

The Virgin Mary, the epitome of faith and trust, submitted herself totally and completely to God's will and, even though she did not yet fully understand the implications of her yes to God, she trusted fully in His providence. This led Elizabeth to proclaim, "Blessed are you who believed that what was spoken to you by the Lord would be fulfilled" (see Luke 1:45). Likewise, let us give our total and unconditional yes to Jesus so that, filled with the same Spirit that overflowed in the heart of Fr. Augustus Tolton, we too may experience the true joy of fruitful intimacy with God.

Songs of Hope in Times of Tribulation

When the people of God come together at the Holy Sacrifice of the Mass, we should not sit back like mere spectators and allow the readings to pass us by while our distracted minds wander elsewhere. We need to walk more closely with Jesus on the road to Emmaus. When the Word of God is proclaimed, we should praise God in our hearts and exclaim with joy, "Did not our hearts burn within us while he talked to us on the road, while he opened to us the Scriptures?" (Luke 24:32). We need to recapture a sense of awe and wonder in listening to and appreciating the depth of God's Word (see Neh. 8:8–10).

> The Church has always venerated the divine Scriptures just as she venerates the body of the Lord, since, especially in the sacred liturgy, she unceasingly receives and offers to the faithful the bread of life from the table both of God's word and of Christ's body. She has always maintained them, and continues to do so, together with sacred tradition, as the supreme rule of faith, since, as inspired by God and committed once and for all to writing, they impart the word of God Himself without change, and make the voice of the Holy Spirit resound in the words of the prophets and Apostles. Therefore, like the Christian religion itself, all the preaching of the Church must be nourished and regulated by Sacred Scripture.[135]

This Spirit-filled joy comes from God's Word, which is not only pages in a book but a Person. St. John in his Gospel says that "in the beginning was the Word, and the Word was with God, and the Word was God.... And the Word became flesh and dwelt among us, full of grace and truth" (John 1:1; 14). In the Word, we don't just read about Jesus; we *encounter* Him. In the Word, we don't just become friends with Jesus; we fall in love with Him. In the Word, we don't simply feel like we are good people; we give our

---

[135] *Sacrosanctum Concilium* 21.

lives to Him. In His goodness and wisdom, God chose to reveal Himself and to make known to us the purpose of His will through Christ, in whom we have access to the Father in the Holy Spirit, and through whom we come to share in the love and life of God.[136]

The psalms are part of the Word of God; they are the liturgical song-prayers of the Church and are used primarily in public prayer: the Mass and the Liturgy of the Hours. Most psalms praise God—for His power and beneficence, for His creation of the world, and for His past acts of deliverance. They envision a world in which everything brought into being by God will praise Him; God, in turn, will hear their prayers and respond to His creation with love and wisdom.

> To sing the psalms with understanding, then, is to meditate on them verse by verse, with the heart always ready to respond in the way the Holy Spirit desires. The one who inspired the psalmist will also be present to those who in faith and love are ready to receive his grace. For this reason the singing of psalms, though it demands the reverence owed to God's majesty, should be the expression of a joyful spirit and a loving heart, in keeping with their character as sacred poetry and divine song and above all with the freedom of the children of God.[137]

Fr. Tolton understood that God is active and alive in the Scriptures and that, especially in the Mass, He wants to feed and nourish us with His Word. "Fr. Tolton's sermons, admonitions, and instructions, always theologically sound, were geared to the intellectual

---

[136] See Vatican Council II, Dogmatic Constitution on Divine Revelation *Dei Verbum* (November 18, 1965), no. 2.

[137] Congregation for Divine Worship, *General Instruction of the Liturgy of the Hours* (February 2, 1971), no. 104, https://www.ewtn.com/library/curia/cdwgilh.htm.

level of his flock."[138] There is no doubt that the long-suffering Tolton family relied on God's word to bring comfort in difficult times, and that the psalms served as a source of hope and consolation. "Though the psalms originated very many centuries ago among an Eastern people, they express accurately the pain and hope, the unhappiness and trust of people of every age and country, and sing above all of faith in God, of revelation, and of redemption."[139]

The psalms are a wellspring of hope, sustenance, and strength for the journey toward eternal life. In my personal life, I have been inspired, challenged, and heartened by the psalms; they have profoundly enriched and blessed my prayer life. There has not been an emotion or feeling, situation or circumstance, problem or concern that I've experienced that is not addressed in the psalms. As I reflect on the life of Fr. Tolton, my mind and heart are drawn to certain selections from the psalms that connect my heart to his. I invite you to pray these yourself: Psalm 13:2–7; Psalm 25:1–5, 17–18; Psalm 37:3–7; Psalm 116:1–8.

A Biblical Parallel: The Cross and the Beatitudes

Mother Teresa once spoke on the relationship between holiness and sacrifice, saying, "A sacrifice to be real must cost, must hurt, and must empty ourselves. Give yourself fully to God. He will use you to accomplish great things on the condition that you believe much more in His love than in your own weakness."[140]

The themes of sacrifice, holiness, and self-gift are abundant both in the psalms and in the life of Fr. Tolton. These scriptural

[138] Hemesath, *Slave to Priest*, 216.
[139] *General Instruction of the Liturgy of the Hours* 107.
[140] Arun Anand, *Indian Nobel Laureates* (New Delhi, India: Ocean Books, 2013), 84.

motifs came alive for me in a very powerful way during a speaking tour of Africa several years ago.

The township of Alexandra, situated about seven miles north of Johannesburg, is one of the poorest areas in all of South Africa. The settlements along the Juskei River, located in dangerous flood plains, have populations that exceed five hundred residents per acre. Alexandra also has a huge number of squatter camps made up of more than thirty-four thousand shacks, which are one-room dwellings made of sheet metal, aluminum, and cardboard, each about thirty-five square feet in size, that house entire families.

The unplanned development and overcrowding make living conditions stressful and unhealthy. Utilities are overloaded, resulting in such low water pressure that three or more families must often share one water source; electrical connections that are haphazard and frequently dangerous; and a sewer system that frequently overflows, spewing waste into the streets. Children have no place to play and are often exposed to diseases caused by exposure to refuse or from vermin that eat their flesh while they sleep. Because of the threat of violent crime, many Alexandrians do not leave their houses at night, even to go to the bathroom. Hence, wastewater is kept in the house overnight and disposed of the next day.

On our way to Alexandra, my host tried to prepare me for what I was about to see, but words could not describe my horror and shock as we made our way through the streets to St. Hubert's Church. In my anxiety, mixed with a bit of Western arrogance, I thought to myself, "What am I doing here?" We pulled into the heavily fortified parish parking lot, and, as I entered the church, my reason for being there became clear: The church was jam-packed. I was surprised that hundreds of parishioners filled the church on a Thursday night; the pastor later told me that each Sunday Mass was just as full.

Before my talk, the pastor asked me to lead Benediction and the Chaplet of Divine Mercy. My feelings of arrogance quickly turned to embarrassment as I saw that the African parishioners knew the Latin prayers better than I did! And the singing was some of the most beautiful and meaningful I have ever heard. Materially, these people had nothing; but spiritually, they had everything!

Every hour of every day, Alexandrians must completely trust in God alone to sustain them. The spiritual strength that enables them to do this flows from the obedience of faith. This is a faith that sees past the pain and suffering of the physical and material world. It is a faith that inspires and enlivens downtrodden people to accept lovingly the heavy crosses they have been given and to see only Jesus, and to find comfort and solace in the wounds of the Savior, with their gaze fixed upon the transcendent joy of the world to come.

The people of Alexandra live in constant fear and have nothing to live on but hope: They are the very people who are dearest to our Lord. Their dire poverty is not by their own choice, but they do choose a *spiritual poverty* that is the absolute realization of their gift from God. The faithful of Alexandra, like the widow of the Gospel who gave all she had (Luke 21:1–4), know well that complete trust in God's providence is born of vulnerability, of not being afraid to break yourself open and pour yourself out in love before the Giver of all gifts.

After my talk, a small reception was held in the parish hall. As I made my way into the room, I was quickly surrounded by a group of teens. They asked me how it was possible to live the truth and beauty of our Catholic Faith in the midst of such debilitating squalor. Some of them had been exposed to satellite television and were starting to seek hope for the future in the materialism of the Western world.

Like a ray of sunlight reflecting off a mirror, I tried to focus their attention on Jesus. I told them that true joy and peace come only from complete surrender to the will of God. I told them that Western civilization, for the most part, has lost her soul — that she has become the prostitute of the culture of death. I told them that the Lord has great things in store for them if they remain faithful to the truths of the Faith and if they willingly become clay in God's hands, letting His warm love mold and shape them into the men and women they are called to be.

I told them that I pray that, when I die, I will have even half their faith. I encouraged them to keep the words of Jesus in the Beatitudes always in their minds (Matt. 5:1–12) and to keep the words of St. Paul close to their hearts. Paul beautifully summarizes the spirituality of Alexandra in his letter to the Corinthians: "[The Lord] said to me, 'My grace is sufficient for you, for my power is made perfect in weakness.' I will all the more gladly boast of my weaknesses, that the power of Christ may rest upon me. For the sake of Christ, then, I am content with weaknesses, insults, hardships, persecutions, and calamities; for when I am weak, then I am strong" (2 Cor. 12:9–10).

The key to understanding the rich blessings of the Beatitudes is acknowledging our dependence on God and saying yes to Christ's invitation to live with Him in the Father and through the Holy Spirit, who fills us with the fire of God's love and ignites the flame of our love in return. And since the love of God embraces all of humanity, we who follow Christ are called to share in His work of salvation in a special way. Living the Beatitudes is our response to God's divine grace in us.

Blessed are the poor in spirit. The poor in spirit are those who acknowledge their spiritual poverty and human frailty, and know how much they need God's help and support. The saints who embody poverty of spirit include Vincent de Paul and Katharine Drexel, who, with heroic faith and love, continued Christ's work of service and charity among those on the margins of society.

Blessed are those who mourn. Those who are in grief or sorrow will be assured of comfort and consolation from the loving, faith-filled community that forms the Body of Christ. What saint can better teach us about the meaning of sorrow than our Blessed Mother? In Luke's Gospel, Simeon says to Mary: "Behold, this child is set for the fall and rising of many in Israel, and for a sign that is spoken against (and a sword will pierce through your own soul also), that thoughts out of many hearts may be revealed" (Luke 2:34–35). The Scriptures are clear: It is through the Immaculate Heart of Mary —through the New Eve—that complete and perfect opposition to sin is established (see Gen. 3:15). It is through the Queen of Heaven, who possesses a genuinely feminine heart of love and is the perfect example of what it means to be fully human, that we find true solace, comfort, and peace.

Blessed are the meek. These are the people who reach out to others in care, compassion, and tenderness, who sacrifice their own needs, and who are constantly aware of the needs of others. The Divine Savior inspired the Dominican friar St. Martin de Porres, who related to everyone with a profound love rooted in pure faith and humility of spirit. St. Martin lovingly comforted the sick and provided food, clothing, and medicine for the poor. His spirit lives on in parents and caretakers who willingly sacrifice themselves for the well-being of an infirm spouse, a disabled child, or an elderly parent. "We think sometimes that poverty is only being hungry, naked and homeless. The poverty of being unwanted, unloved, and uncared for is the greatest poverty."[141]

Blessed are those who hunger and thirst for righteousness. These saints among us work to ensure that everyone receives the opportunity to live a life of dignity and self-respect. Often, the price they pay to follow Jesus is very high. Sts. Teresa Benedicta of the

---

[141] Rev. Matthew R. Mauriello, *Mercies Remembered: Reflections and Reminiscences of a Parish Priest* (Maitland, FL: Xulon Press, 2010), 278.

Cross (Edith Stein) and Maximilian Kolbe paid the ultimate price under the Nazi regime, and today police officers, firefighters, and other public-safety professionals know that the greatest gift they can give is to lay their lives on the line—and even to sacrifice their lives—so that others may live.

Blessed are the merciful. These are the ones who extend compassion and forgiveness to all around them. St. Louis IX, the French king who was a great lover of justice, was renowned for his charity. Beggars ate from his table, and St. Louis himself often ate their leftovers. He washed the feet of the wretched, ministered to lepers, and daily provided food for more than one hundred poor people throughout his kingdom. St. Louis founded many hospitals and established houses for reformed prostitutes and the blind. Imagine what kind of world it would be if our political leaders followed his example!

Blessed are the pure in heart. For these saints, God's presence in every person and experience is simply obvious; they are described as being able to see God. This beatitude helps us to remove prejudice and bias so that we can see others as God sees them. As St. Teresa of Calcutta so beautifully reminds us: "Let us touch the dying, the poor, the lonely and the unwanted according to the graces we have received, and let us not be ashamed or slow to do the humble work."[142]

Blessed are the peacemakers. These are people who help to break down the barriers that divide people. The Father sent His Son to break down the walls between Him and His people, and sometimes even between the people themselves. St. Francis of Assisi, the founder of the Franciscan Order and a permanent deacon,

---

[142] Tracy Maxwell, *Being Single, with Cancer: A Solo Survivor's Guide to Life, Love, Health, and Happiness* (New York: Demos Medical Publishing, 2014), 97.

understood that his role was to assist the bishop with his mission of evangelization and to help the faithful grow in holiness. Through his sanctifying ministry of teaching and leadership, the deacon reaches out to the poor and the marginalized, the fallen-away Catholic, and the family in crisis, with the message of the gospel and, like the friends of the paralytic on the stretcher, brings people to Jesus (Luke 5:17–26).

Blessed are those who are persecuted for righteousness' sake. Blessed indeed are those who, in the defense of the beauty of our Faith, have the fortitude and strength to put the values of truth, love, and justice for all above their own survival. The Ugandan martyrs, for example, were dismembered, burned, beheaded, castrated, and fed to wild animals for protecting young boys from a violent, pedophile king.

Blessed are you when men revile you and persecute you and utter all kinds of evil against you falsely on my account. We are called to preach the gospel in its fullness — not just the parts we like! This means that when we live our Faith every day, simply through the witness of our lives — when we seek peace instead of war; when we defend the right to life for all human beings from the moment of conception until natural death; when we defend the dignity of marriage and family life; and when we take concrete steps to heal the wounds of racism — we will be persecuted, mocked, ridiculed, and scorned, just as Christ was as He made His way to Calvary. Life is too short for us to worry about what other people think. We are called by God to be saints: to live our Faith with courage and conviction in this time and in this place, and to put all our trust in Him. As the Scriptures encourage us, "In God alone be at rest, my soul; for my hope comes from Him. He alone is my rock, my stronghold, my fortress; I stand firm" (Ps. 62:6–7). We are to rejoice and be glad, for our reward will be great in Heaven!

In the Beatitudes, Christ reveals the kind of people we are all called to be. These are the qualities that made the saints and that will make us saints as well. The Beatitudes form a foundation for holiness and make clear what is expected of a follower of Jesus. They point to our participation in the Kingdom of Heaven here on earth: a society that exists according to the values of truth and love, of compassion and mercy, of peace and freedom—all qualities that flow from the very heart of God Himself.

Saints are people who have responded generously to the love of God showered upon them. They have survived the pains and challenges of this world; they have lived the Beatitudes; they have washed their robes white in the blood of the Lamb; and now they rejoice and share in the victory of Christ (Rev. 7:14). Strengthened by the Food of the Angels that we receive from the sacred altar at every Mass, let us say, "Blessing and glory and wisdom and thanksgiving and honor and power and might be to our God for ever and ever! Amen" (Rev. 7:12).

Chapter 5

A Culture of Life and the
Meaning of Human Suffering

A Culture of Life

The challenges facing society and families today are of the same basic three types as those faced by Fr. Tolton is his day, through their complexion has changed: material or physical (e.g., substance abuse, violent crime, human trafficking, and absent fathers), philosophical (e.g., moral relativism, gender neutrality, and subjective truth), and spiritual (e.g., racism, atheism, and agnosticism). These broad groupings and the wide-ranging issues within them are not mutually exclusive.

The Church's mission to share the life-changing news of the encounter with Jesus—to go and make disciples for Christ—comes into conflict with a secular system that claims there is no objective reality independent of human subjectivity and reasoning. As a result, those who engage in evangelization are perceived by society to be dangerous threats to the supreme good of enlightened modernism: "tolerance" and "diversity."

Imbued with and inspired by the spirit of Fr. Tolton, we must challenge the pernicious influence of contemporary culture by building upon the solid foundation of our Faith—a Faith that forms the heart and soul of our spiritual identity as Catholics. We must respond with courage, conviction, and unwavering faith to our baptismal call to holiness in order to answer Christ's directive to be "perfect as your heavenly Father is perfect" (Matt. 5:48). In turn, we can "shoulder the responsibility laid upon us by our Baptism into the Body of Christ. This responsibility is to proclaim our faith and to take an active part in building up the Church."[143]

Fr. Augustus spent his life faithfully serving the Church, principally in ministry to the black Catholic community and others who were on the periphery of society. In the face of the challenges confronting our Church today, combating only *specific aspects* of prevailing material, philosophical, and spiritual errors without working to deconstruct the *comprehensive framework* that supports and undergirds the entire corrupt structure will render any long-term, permanent solutions weak and ineffective. Our job, rather, is to replace it with a holistic Christian anthropology rooted in the objective truth of the natural law.

For example, unraveling the tangled web of racism, while extremely important work, cannot be the sole response to the institutional dehumanization that marks our modern culture, since "solving" racism *alone* cannot answer the deeper, more serious questions that need to be explored: Are we so preoccupied and distracted with worldly ideology that we fail to notice what is happening to our children, who, in the midst of a cultural onslaught, opt for no religious affiliation at all? Why have street gangs and drug cartels replaced families? Where are our husbands and fathers to lead and guide the next generation?

Racism is learned behavior. Overturning it cannot be just about some abstract notions concerning the culture or some nefarious outside force. We have to look within our communities, indeed, within our very selves.

---

[143] Howze, *What We Have Seen and Heard*, 18.

For white Catholics, that means thinking carefully about the way racial issues are spoken about: Children especially pick up on even subtle disparaging or otherwise prejudiced remarks, and they learn from them. It means actively choosing to treat people of color—especially fellow worshippers—with equal dignity and respect. And although combating racism cannot be a purely internal act, reforming and converting the mind and soul always to see others in the image and likeness of God is essential.

But, and this is extremely important, black Catholic communities have responsibilities, too. Ideologies that present black Americans only as victims are dangerous and infantilizing—and do not respect Fr. Tolton's legacy. He encouraged his flock to bear wrongs patiently, yes, but also to see to it that their own houses were in order. The black Catholic community must be a force for reform and conversion in families and souls as much as—if not more than—it is a salve for the external pressures of racism. In fact, this is part of combating racism.

In other words, proclaiming with our lives that Jesus Christ is Lord—living in holiness and purity of heart, and being completely vulnerable before God's love and will every day—is the catalyst for change; it is the sledgehammer that destroys the material, philosophical, and spiritual constructs that constrain and oppress us. We must rediscover the beauty of our Catholic tradition and renew our commitment to live the teachings of our Faith with boldness, fidelity, and enthusiasm! "For those who live according to the flesh set their minds on the things of the flesh, but those who live according to the Spirit set their minds on the things of the Spirit. To set the mind on the flesh is death, but to set the mind on the Spirit is life and peace" (Rom. 8:5–6).

The secular framework that needs to be dismantled can be summed up in one phrase, popularized by Pope St. John Paul II: the culture of death. This is a serious challenge for the entire Body of Christ, but it has particular import for the communities today who were served by Fr. Tolton.

"Historically, children were always welcomed in African American families, no matter the circumstances surrounding the pregnancy. Tragically, that tradition is changing before our very eyes. The Centers for Disease Control and Prevention reports that Black women are about twelve percent of the female population, but account for thirty-five percent of all abortions."[144] According to census data for the year 2000, abortion has eliminated between fourteen and fifteen million black Americans since 1973, a total equal to the combined population of eight Midwestern states. "Abortion is shrinking our churches, schools, communities and congressional districts, as well as our future."[145]

According to the harrowing documentary *MAAFA 21*, "Since 1993, legal abortion has killed more African Americans than AIDS, cancer, diabetes, heart disease, and violent crime combined. Every week, more blacks die in American abortion clinics than were killed in the entire Vietnam War."[146] The purveyors of the culture of death want us to embrace their eugenic ideology as status quo. They would like us to ignore the fact that abortion "kills as many African American people every four days as the Ku Klux Klan killed in 150 years."[147] The purveyors of subjective truth want to convince us that abortion and euthanasia are merely political or civil "rights"

---

[144] Michelle Williams, "Abortion and the Black Community," lecture given at the National Black Catholic Convocation I, Indianapolis, Indiana, April 21, 2004.

[145] Gloria Purvis, "What Will It Take to Respect Life in the Black Community?," lecture given at the National Black Catholic Convocation I, Indianapolis, Indiana, April 21, 2004.

[146] Excerpt from the DVD *MAAFA 21: Black Genocide in the 21st Century* (Denton, TX: Life Dynamics, 2009).

[147] Ibid.

issues. In reality, marketing slogans such as "low-income health care," "reproductive rights," and "family planning" are simply euphemisms used by those who are trying to exterminate unborn and defenseless human beings as if they were vermin.

As a community of believers in Jesus Christ, black Catholics do a great job of raising awareness about important issues such as poverty, affirmative action, racism, and civil rights, but if we continue to kill ourselves through this egregious abuse of our freedom, there will not be enough of us around for anyone to notice. When we allow abortion, we actually assist in and encourage the elimination of our brothers and sisters, something that hate groups could not accomplish for decades in this country.[148] For true followers of Christ, and indeed for all people of goodwill, abortion is not about opinion or choice: It is a matter of life and death.

Life and Death

Fr. Tolton endured a lifetime of racial animosity and hatred. Even after his ordination to the priesthood, and despite the fact that he was adored by Catholics both black and white, some of his fellow clergyman openly referred to him as the "nigger priest."

> On more than one occasion Fr. Weiss, in no uncertain terms, told Fr. Tolton that he was expected to minister only to blacks; he told him bluntly that he should order the white people out of his church.... Fr. Weiss ... avowed publicly that the money collected from the white people attending St. Joseph's Church [Fr. Tolton's parish] belonged to their own parishes and even insinuated that attendance at the black church was not valid in the case of white Catholics.[149]

[148] Ibid.
[149] Hemesath, *Slave to Priest*, 183.

Fr. Augustus Tolton

The tenacity and dedication of clerics such as Fr. Tolton allowed African American families to grow and flourish in the midst of racism and poverty. In the years after Fr. Tolton's death, however, efforts to undermine black family life continued — including movements to convince black Americans to contribute to their own demise through so-called "family planning" programs.

Many Americans are unaware of Margaret Sanger's Negro Project. Sanger created this program in 1939, with the aim to restrict — many believe exterminate — the black population. Margaret Sanger aligned herself with the eugenicists whose ideology prevailed in the early 20th century. Eugenicists strongly espoused racial supremacy and "purity," particularly of the "Aryan" race. Eugenicists hoped to purify the bloodlines and improve the race by encouraging the "fit" to reproduce and the "unfit" to restrict their reproduction. They sought to contain the "inferior" races through segregation, sterilization, birth control and abortion. Sanger … argued for birth control using the "scientifically verified" threat of poverty, sickness, racial tension and overpopulation as its background. Sanger's publication, *The Birth Control Review* (founded in 1917) regularly published pro-eugenic articles from eugenicists, such as Ernst Rudin.[150]

Sanger institutionalized her work in the form of the American Birth Control League, the forerunner of Planned Parenthood. She lamented the burden of "human waste" on society.

---

[150] George Grant, *Grand Illusions: The Legacy of Planned Parenthood*, 2nd ed. (Franklin, TN: Adroit Press, 1992), 95–96. Rudin worked as Adolf Hitler's director of genetic sterilization and founded the Nazi Society for Racial Hygiene.

It [charity] encourages the healthier and more normal sections of the world to shoulder the burden of unthinking and indiscriminate fecundity of others; which brings with it, as I think the reader must agree, a dead weight of human waste. Instead of decreasing and aiming to eliminate the stocks that are most detrimental to the future of the race and the world, it tends to render them to a menacing degree dominant.[151]

She concluded:

The most serious charge that can be brought against modern "benevolence" is that it encourages the perpetuation of defectives, delinquents and dependents. These are the most dangerous elements in the world community, the most devastating curse on human progress and expression.[152]

In a 1926 address , Sanger said:

It now remains for the United States government to set a sensible example to the world by offering a bonus or yearly pension to all obviously unfit parents who allow themselves to be sterilized by harmless and scientific means. In this way the moron and the diseased would have no posterity to inherit their unhappy condition. The number of the feeble-minded would decrease and a heavy burden would be lifted from the shoulders of the fit.[153]

---

[151] Margaret Sanger, *The Pivot of Civilization* (New York: Brentano's, 1922), 116–117.

[152] Ibid., 123.

[153] Margaret Sanger, "The Function of Sterilization," *Birth Control Review* (October 1926): 299. Sanger delivered the address before the Institute of Euthenics at Vassar College on August 5, 1926.

Fr. Augustus Tolton

"Sanger suggested the answer to poverty and degradation lay in smaller numbers of blacks [and] built the work of Planned Parenthood on the ideas and resources of the eugenics movement under the pretense of 'better health' and 'family planning.'"[154]

As a former slave who served many descendants from Africa, Fr. Tolton was keenly aware that African spirituality (generally speaking) is characterized by four principal elements: the intense awareness of always being in the presence of God; worship involving the whole person, body and soul; joy that is deep, passionate, vibrant, and emotional; and a deep sense of community where the "I" finds meaning in the "we." The Church has, in Africa and in this country, molded this spirituality into beautiful expressions of the true religion; soulless organizations like Planned Parenthood have always seen that spirituality as a problem to be overcome.

> Sanger knew blacks were a religious people — and how useful ministers would be to her project. She wrote in [a letter regarding the Negro Project that] "the minister's work is also important and he should be trained … as to our ideals and the goal that we hope to reach. We do not want word to go out that we want to exterminate the Negro population, and the minister is the man who can straighten out that idea if it ever occurs to any of their more rebellious members."[155]

The "education" mission of Planned Parenthood extended to all areas of black life and culture. One of Sanger's supporters, Dr. Dorothy Ferebee, gave a talk in which she said, "The future program

---

[154] Tanya L. Green, "The Negro Project: Margaret Sanger's Eugenic Plan for Black Americans," Concerned Women for America, May 1, 2001, https://concernedwomen.org/the-negro-project-margaret-sangers-eugenic-plan-for-black-americans/.

[155] Ibid.

[of Planned Parenthood] should center around more education in the field through the work of a professional Negro worker, because those of us who believe that the benefits of Planned Parenthood as a vital key to the elimination of human waste must reach the entire population."[156] "She peppered her speech with the importance of Negro professionals, fully integrated into the [Planned Parenthood] staff,... who could interpret the program and objectives to [other blacks] in the normal course of day-to-day contacts; could break down fallacious attitudes and beliefs and elements of distrust; could inspire the confidence of the group; and would not be suspect of the intent to eliminate the race."[157]

Following Fr. Tolton's witness and example, we must rise up —even in the face of discrimination and rejection—and take the lead in building a culture that respects all human life from its creation until natural death, armed with the sword of genuine Christian love in one hand and the shield of objective truth in the other. We must not be afraid to speak the truth in love (see Eph. 4:15), the most fundamental truth being that "human life must be respected and protected absolutely from the moment of conception. From the first moment of existence, a human being must be recognized as having the rights of a person—among which is the sacred right of every innocent being to life."[158]

This is not a suggestion. Our Lord says, "If any man would come after me, let him deny himself and take up his cross and follow me. For whoever would save his life will lose it, and whoever loses his life for my sake will find it. For what will it profit a man, if he gains the whole world and forfeits his life?" (Matt. 16:24–26; cf. Mark

---

[156] Dr. Dorothy Ferebee, "Planned Parenthood as a Public Health for the Negro Race," BCFA Annual Meeting, January 29, 1942, 3.

[157] Green, "The Negro Project."

[158] CCC 2270; cf. CDF, *Donum vitae* I,1.

8:34–35; Luke 9:23–24). This is what it means to abandon the thinking of the world and to follow Christ as His disciples. When we pick up our cross and follow Jesus, vocations to the priesthood and consecrated religious life will increase, since these vocations will be fostered in the domestic church, where the family—led by strong, faith-filled fathers and mothers—will become the primary vehicle of evangelization.

Fr. Tolton understood well that religious vocations are the fruit of a culture of life rooted in the family. Even though the cross of racism weighed heavily on his shoulders, he acknowledged, "It was the priests of the Church who taught me to pray and to forgive my persecutors. It was through the direction of a [nun] that I . . . beheld for the first time the glimmering light of truth and the majesty of the Church."[159] The consecrated religious of Fr. Tolton's time "bore eloquent witness to the power of the Holy Spirit accomplishing the work of spiritual freedom even in the moment of physical oppression." Drawing from this wellspring, in the words of St. John Paul II, "religious today offer a comparable witness to the Church and society, proclaiming God's Kingdom to a world shackled by consumerism, mindless pleasure-seeking and irresponsible individualism—shackles of the spirit which are even more destructive than the chains of physical slavery. . . . Surely that spirit can be found [by embracing the richness of our] spiritual and cultural heritage. The inspiration we draw from the great men and women of our past will allow our young people to see the value of a strong family life."[160] You reap what you sow: The seeds of fidelity and truth sown in the church of the home will yield a bountiful harvest of workers in the Lord's vineyard.

---

[159] Hemesath, *Slave to Priest*, 185.

[160] Pope John Paul II, Meeting with the black Catholics of New Orleans (September 12, 1987), nos. 2, 4.

In every age there have been men and women who, obedient to the Father's call and to the prompting of the Spirit, have chosen this special way of following Christ, in order to devote themselves to him with an "undivided" heart (cf. 1 Corinthians 7:34). Like the Apostles, they too have left everything behind in order to be with Christ and to put themselves, as he did, at the service of God and their brothers and sisters. In this way, through the many charisms of spiritual and apostolic life bestowed on them by the Holy Spirit, they have helped to make the mystery and mission of the Church shine forth, and in doing so have contributed to the renewal of society.[161]

In the spirit of Fr. Augustus Tolton, let us work to foster vocations to the priesthood, diaconate, and religious life in our own families, parishes, and communities. Inspired by the first black priest in America, I offer a few suggestions on how to create an environment in the home where children consider that God may be calling them to consecrated life.

1. *Ask your children to consider a religious vocation.* One evening during our family's movie and pizza night, as we were watching *The Sound of Music*, I jokingly asked one of my daughters—the one who I never thought would have a vocation—if she ever considered religious life. To my astonishment, she said that she had! This reminded me that, as Catholic parents, my wife and I have a responsibility to spend time discussing possible religious vocations with our children, just as my own mother supported and encouraged me as a teenager when I was discerning a call to the Benedictines.

---

[161] Pope John Paul II, Apostolic Exhortation *Vita Consecrata: On the Consecrated Life and Its Mission in the Church and in the World* (March 25, 1996), no. 1.

Teaching our children to love the sound of God's voice is the first Greatest Commandment.

Hear, O Israel: The Lord our God is one Lord; and you shall love the Lord your God with all your heart, and with all your soul, and with all your might. And these words which I command you this day shall be upon your heart; *and you shall teach them diligently to your children, and shall talk of them when you sit in your house, and when you walk by the way, and when you lie down, and when you rise.* And you shall bind them as a sign upon your hand, and they shall be as frontlets between your eyes. *And you shall write them on the doorposts of your house* and on your gates. (Deut. 6:4–9, emphasis added)

2. *Pray for vocations to religious life as a family.* Families should pray with and for each other every day, and those prayers should include men and women who are discerning a call to priesthood or religious life. At grace before meals, for example, you can add the following prayer: "We ask, O Lord, that You let more men and women hear the call to serve You as a priest, brother, or sister. Amen." Dinner is also a great opportunity for family members to talk about a priest, brother, or sister who has meant something to them — perhaps someone who taught them in school or visited them in the hospital.

3. *Encourage your children to speak with a priest or religious about his or her vocation.* A great way to do this is to invite your local priest, or a religious brother or sister, to your home for a family dinner. The witness of their priestly or monastic attire will impact your children and will provide a great opportunity for your kids to ask questions and for your guest to share his or her vocation story.

4. *If your parish has a vocations committee, learn about its activities and participate in at least one program.* Maybe some of your fellow

parishioners are involved with the Serrans,[162] an international lay apostolate dedicated to fostering and affirming vocations to the priesthood and vowed religious life. If the parish does not have a vocations committee, it might support apostolates such as Vocation Boom,[163] whose work is focused on building a culture that is open to the priesthood. Keep an eye out, also, for Third Orders or Oblates—laypersons or ordained ministers who incorporate the spirituality of a particular religious order into their daily lives.[164] These are great ways that the Body of Christ can work together to open the pathway of discernment in the hearts and minds of our children.

5. *Discover a ministry in your area that is sponsored by a religious community.* Go with your children to visit a local religious community for prayers and a meal. Volunteer at a school run by a religious order. Actively participate in the ministerial work of the order, such as feeding the homeless, providing resources for pregnant teenagers, or giving a loving welcome to those who are finding their way back to the Faith.

6. *Support diocesan efforts that promote vocation discernment.* Many dioceses now have Quo Vadis Days[165] as well as vocation retreats or discernment weekends. Many dioceses also support Newman Centers on college and university campuses.

7. *Include ten minutes for silent reading of Sacred Scripture daily.* Offer this time for the intention of those considering the priesthood or consecrated life.

---

[162] Visit their website: http://www.serrainternational.org/.

[163] Visit their website: https://www.vocationboom.com/.

[164] I myself am a Benedictine oblate, which means I follow the Rule of St. Benedict and integrate Benedictine spirituality into every aspect of my life. Others do the same as part of Third Orders (another name for oblates) in a variety of religious orders, such as the Dominicans, Franciscans, Carmelites, and so forth.

[165] *Quo Vadis* is Latin for "Where are you going?" Visit the Quo Vadis Days website: http://qvdays.org/.

Fr. Augustus Tolton

8. *Pray in Adoration before the Blessed Sacrament for religious vocations.* Eucharistic Adoration is a game changer! People who participate in Eucharistic Adoration experience the power of repentance and conversion, leading to deeper intimacy with Christ. Adoration fosters greater reverence at Mass, an expanded desire for personal holiness, and a stronger sense of union with the parish and the whole Church. Since the early centuries of Christianity, the Church has linked Eucharistic devotion with service to the poor. In my experience, parishes and families who practice Adoration of the Blessed Sacrament have seen an increase in vocations to the priesthood, diaconate, and religious life.

Fr. Tolton was encouraged in his vocation by his mother, and by faithful priests and religious sisters, in whom, through "the profession of the evangelical counsels [poverty, chastity and obedience], the characteristic features of Jesus ... are made constantly 'visible' in the midst of the world, and the eyes of the faithful are directed towards the mystery of the Kingdom of God already at work in history, even as it awaits its full realization in heaven."[166] Our priests and consecrated religious live the reality of the wedding feast of the Lamb (see Rev. 19:9) right here on earth. They are tangible, visible signs of the heavenly reality of the Beatific Vision who allow us a glimpse into our future glory as we await "our blessed hope, the appearing of the glory of our great God and Savior, Jesus Christ" (Titus 2:13).

Crucified with Christ

As Jesus died on the Cross while being mocked by those who condemned Him, Our Lord poured Himself out in complete and perfect love. Jesus calls us to love as He loves, for it is in the

---

[166] Pope John Paul II, *Vita Consecrata* 1.

crucified Christ that the true meaning of forgiveness and freedom are revealed.

We learned much about the meaning of suffering from St. John Paul II's beautiful example during the last years of his pontificate. The Holy Father showed us that there is a profound and indissoluble link between sharing in the Cross of Christ and sharing in the Kingdom of Christ. Man suffers with Christ, and, for the sake of his own redemption and the redemption of others, he is thereby brought closer to Christ. The Redeemer is active in him, and the power of the Risen Lord enables him to suffer and to share in His Crucifixion, Passion, and Death. When he suffers with Christ now, man knows that he will one day share in the Resurrection. Suffering with and in Christ is suffering for the sake of bringing about God's Kingdom:

> To the prospect of the Kingdom of God is linked hope in that glory which has its beginning in the Cross of Christ. The Resurrection revealed this glory — eschatological glory — which, in the Cross of Christ, was completely obscured by the immensity of suffering. Those who share in the sufferings of Christ are also called, through their own sufferings, to share in *glory*. Paul expresses this in various places. To the Romans he writes: "We are ... fellow heirs with Christ, provided we suffer with him in order that we may also be glorified with him. I consider that the sufferings of this present time are not worth comparing with the glory that is to be revealed in us". In the Second Letter to the Corinthians we read: "For this slight momentary affliction is preparing for us an eternal weight of glory beyond all comparison, because we look not to the things that are seen but to things that are unseen". The Apostle Peter will express this truth in the following words of his First Letter: "But rejoice in so

far as you share Christ's sufferings, that you may also rejoice and be glad when his glory is revealed".[167]

God has allowed man to suffer, but He has *graced* man with the ability to suffer *through Jesus*. Through the Passion and Death of Christ, man is made a son and daughter of God in Baptism. There is, then, a cooperation between God and man that can be truly realized only in a loving relationship of communion, to which God calls man through suffering. This cooperation happens by grace; the only thing that man contributes is his freely willed fiat in submission to God's holy will. The work of salvation belongs to God alone, but man has a role through this cooperation, which is why he can talk about being made worthy of the dignity of the Kingdom.

Suffering, no matter how deep or profound it is, can be related to the Cross of Christ and can be used as a way of deepening the experience of God's merciful love. Redemption is not a pure substitution: Christ did not suffer so that man would not have to. Rather, Jesus suffered for us to enable us to love as He loves. Through the Cross, we can participate in Christ's suffering. He suffered to make more fully ours what He has accomplished—union with the Father. Christ surrendered Himself wholly to the Father and carried out His plan of salvation. What Christ has *objectively* accomplished has to be *subjectively* appropriated by man, and his free embrace of suffering acts as one of the means of this appropriation. Man can take his suffering and, by uniting himself with Christ, be brought back to the Father. Thus, man can share in Jesus' own communion with the Father in a way that he could not before:

[167] Pope John Paul II, Apostolic Letter *Salvifici Doloris* (February 11, 1984), no. 22.

A Culture of Life and the Meaning of Human Suffering

As a result of Christ's salvific work, man exists on earth *with the hope* of eternal life and holiness. And even though the victory over sin and death achieved by Christ in his Cross and Resurrection does not abolish temporal suffering from human life, nor free from suffering the whole historical dimension of human existence, it nevertheless *throws a new light* upon this dimension and upon every suffering: the light of salvation. This is the light of the Gospel, that is, of the Good News. At the heart of this light is the truth expounded in the conversation with Nicodemus: "For God so loved the world that he gave his only Son". This truth radically changes the picture of man's history and his earthly situation: in spite of the sin that took root in this history both as an original inheritance and as the "sin of the world" and as the sum of personal sins, God the Father has loved the only-begotten Son, that is, he loves him in a lasting way; and then in time, precisely through this all-surpassing love, he "gives" this Son, that he may strike at the very roots of human evil and thus draw close in a salvific way to the whole world of suffering in which man shares.[168]

The complete answer to the question of suffering will be found only in Christ, because it is only in the full revelation of divine love that man finds the truth. Suffering is an expression, ultimately, of His love. In His infinite wisdom, God knows that by allowing man to abuse his freedom and, as a consequence, to bring suffering into the world, He is able to bring a greater good out of it. By sharing with others the love God pours out for the suffering, man becomes an agent of His merciful love in the alleviation of further suffering. By embracing suffering himself and alleviating it in others, man

---

[168] Ibid., no. 15.

becomes like Jesus: He grows closer to the Father and is able to participate more fully in the Father's life.

All human suffering has been redeemed by Christ on the Cross. No human suffering, then, remains utterly pointless or meaningless:

> In order to perceive the true answer to the "why" of suffering, we must look to the revelation of divine love, the ultimate source of the meaning of everything that exists. Love is also the richest source of the meaning of suffering, which always remains a mystery: we are conscious of the insufficiency and inadequacy of our explanations. Christ causes us to enter into the mystery and to discover the "why" of suffering, as far as we are capable of grasping the sublimity of divine love.
>
> In order to discover the profound meaning of suffering, following the revealed word of God, we must open ourselves wide to the human subject in his manifold potentiality. We must above all accept the light of Revelation not only insofar as it expresses the transcendent order of justice but also insofar as it illuminates this order with Love, as the definitive source of everything that exists. Love is also the fullest source of the answer to the question of the meaning of suffering. This answer has been given by God to man in the Cross of Jesus Christ.[169]

Fr. Tolton's life teaches us that sometimes God humbles us in order to exalt us, and that He uses our limitations and weakness to show forth his majesty (see 1 Sam. 2:7). In his suffering, Fr. Tolton reminds us that living in the heart of God means uniting ourselves to the Cross of Christ. He shows us that the journey of faith starts with each one of us living, acting, and being in a way that says yes to God's truth and love.

[169] Pope John Paul II, *Salvifici Doloris* 13.

Going Forward in Hope

We are all called to live in Christ: to follow Him, to carry the Cross, to pour ourselves out, to sacrifice ourselves in love, and to forgive. Fr. Tolton gave himself completely to the Church in response to God's invitation to share in His life and love. He is a role model for all those who seek to be configured more perfectly to Christ.

This humble priest shows us all that being made in God's image and likeness brings with it a tremendous responsibility of love and communion rooted in the obedience of faith. To obey in faith means to listen to God's voice and allow that voice to change our lives. Fr. Tolton's life bears witness to the truth that, when we freely, willingly, and lovingly place all our trust in God, then we will find true happiness and peace.

A Biblical Parallel: The Gospel of Life

During the presentation in the Temple, Simeon predicted that Jesus would become a sign of contradiction (Luke 2:34). Our Lord teaches His disciples today that those whom He came to save are to share in the pain, suffering, and rejection that Jesus endured for the sake of the gospel—but that their ultimate happiness and great reward will be life with God forever. These, then, are the "Blessed": the poor, the hungry, and the sorrowing who, in spite of their physical and spiritual condition, recognize how deeply God loves them! The blessed also include those who are hated, insulted, and denounced simply because they have the courage to take a stand for Jesus.

The blessed are those who are not afraid to think with the heart and the mind of the Church because objective truth will always triumph over the truth we create for ourselves. The Church has taught, for example, that destroying embryos—who are human beings at the earliest stage of development—for the purpose of harvesting stem cells is always morally objectionable and evil. The living human embryo is a human person with his or her own identity. From this it follows that, as human beings, they have a right to their own lives. "Every human being owes his existence to the love of God, and only the love of husband and wife constitutes a mediation of that love in conformity with the plan of the Creator."[170]

And science has proven the wisdom of the Church: There are places from which stem cells can be licitly obtained without violating the dignity of the human person, such as from skin, from umbilical cord blood, and from bone marrow. And when the State of California, for instance, handed out nearly $230 million dollars to fourteen research teams tasked with developing new stem cell therapies—ten of the fourteen projects involved *adult stem cells exclusively.* You may have heard that *only* embryonic stem cells hold the potential for life-saving cures, but that's simply not true!

The Church teaches that any research that does not raise significant ethical problems, particularly adult stem cell research, should be encouraged and supported. But you cannot create children in a laboratory, kill them, and then use their genes for research, no matter how noble that research may be. Using human embryos for medical experimentation is not simply morally unacceptable; it is barbaric.

In our battle to preserve and defend the rights of all human beings to exist, let us arm ourselves with the weapons of strength, love, and wisdom in the Spirit. Our strength, which comes from God, is rooted in love and gives us the faith and courage to bear hardships for the gospel. None of us enjoys suffering, and as followers of

---

[170] Congregation for the Doctrine of the Faith, Instruction *Dignitatis Personae* on Certain Bioethical Questions (June 20, 2008), nos. 28–33.

Christ and witnesses of truth, we cannot sit idly by as others suffer and die all around us.

Every Sunday, we profess our faith in God the Father, the Almighty; in Jesus Christ, the only Son of God; and in the Holy Spirit, the Lord and Giver of life. The Creed reminds us of who we are and what we believe. But sometimes—when life throws us a curveball and we are faced with personal challenges or stressful family situations—we become afraid to pick up our cross and follow Jesus. While looking directly into the face of a culture of death, it is not easy to respect and stand up for the gift of life given to us by God.

A few years back, I was delighted to hear that some college friends were expecting their fifth child. But my joy quickly turned to sorrow when I read the first line of the e-mail: "It started as a routine ultrasound." They quickly learned that their daughter had anencephaly, a neural tube disorder in which the skull is not properly formed and much of the brain is missing.

They started a blog and posted updates about how things were going. A month after the ultrasound, they wrote:

A question that comes up is, "How do you deal with a situation like this?" How many times have we been asked already if we would like to terminate. It is not at all an option for us. This is our child that we are going to love and nurture for as long as we can. Actually, she isn't even our child ultimately: she is God's child. Like all of our children. Our deep faith in God and our hope in heaven keep us going.[171]

These friends took the words of Our Lord seriously, opening their hearts wide to allow God's truth to live in them: "I am the

---

[171] See *Eisenbacher Family Blog—Baby*, November 7, 2005, entry, http://sites.onlinemac.com/eisenbacherfamily/baby.html.

vine, you are the branches. He who abides in me, and I in him, he it is that bears much fruit, for apart from me you can do nothing" (John 15:5). These courageous parents allowed God the Father to prune away the brittle branches of the culture of death.

My friends named their daughter Angela because they knew she was going to be their little angel in Heaven. They had been praying for a miracle, and, just after the New Year, they wrote: "Dear Lord, if not a miracle healing, then please let her be born alive so we can shower our love on her." A child first learns to love in his mother's womb, where he knows that the relationship of love and life is intensely personal. Like the branch attached to the vine, the child is literally attached to his mother, depending on her love for his very life. Jesus says to us, "As a branch cannot bear fruit by itself, unless it abides in the vine, neither can you, unless you abide in me" (John 15:4). We depend on the love of God for our very life, and He invites us to live according to His will so that we can bear much fruit.

When Angela was born, she weighed six pounds, seven ounces. Her parents thought they would have only a few minutes with her, but she lived for three days. During that time, Angela learned the meaning of love from her mother's gentle touch as she nursed from her mother's breast. The child experienced the love of God through a unique and special bond—a bond no man can appreciate or understand.

"If you abide in me, and my words abide in you, ask whatever you will, and it shall be done for you" (John 15:7). On the third day, Angela's breathing became labored, and she started to turn purple. Surrounded by family and friends, Angela took her last breath, opening her eyes briefly as she slipped away—the only time she opened them her whole life. Parents' primary responsibility is to get their children to Heaven, and God blessed these parents for a job well done by allowing Angela to gaze upon the faces of her father and mother, who sacrificed so much and who remained firmly joined to the vine of Christ.

Angela's story reminds us that certain Church teachings in the areas of faith and morals can never change, regardless of whether people accept them or are faithful to them.[172] We as Christians cannot accept the Jiminy Cricket philosophy of "let your conscience be your guide," which "suggests that we are responsibly following our conscience when we knowingly replace Christ's teaching with the world's opinions."[173] If we want to free ourselves from the slavery of the culture of death, we must come before Jesus. We must remove ourselves from the darkness and confusion of sin so that the light of God's life and truth can shine brightly upon us.

The prevailing attitude in our culture treats suffering like a disease that needs to be eradicated at any cost. We ignore the truth that all human suffering has been redeemed by Christ on the Cross and is therefore capable of being used as the means of encountering and experiencing God's merciful love. No human suffering remains meaningless.

Killing human beings can never be an answer to suffering, no matter how great that suffering may be. We exist not to avoid suffering, but to find meaning in the suffering that is unavoidable. A truly compassionate response to a mother who has found out that her child has a genetic illness [or to an elderly person who has a terminal disease] is not to kill them, but to create a society that welcomes and cares for [them: mother, child, grandparent]. We must strive for

---

[172] See Most Rev. Samuel J. Aquila, D.D., *You Will Know the Truth and the Truth Will Set You Free: A Pastoral Letter on Deepening our Understanding of the Truths of the Catholic Faith* (November 30, 2004), no. 7, https://www.ewtn.com/library/bishops/truthfre.htm
[173] Ibid.

a society that values all human life, and does not seek the easy way out through the destruction of human life.[174]

The Gospel tells us what Christ expects from each of His followers: to do our duty as faithful servants. Sometimes this means being unpopular. Sometimes this means standing up for truth when it is easier to live a lie. Sometimes this means bearing our share of hardships for the gospel with the strength that comes from God (see 2 Tim. 1:8). It always means asking ourselves, "Have I become so used to living in a culture of death that goodness, beauty, and truth are only noble ideas and no longer a way of life?"

We are called to be in the world but not of the world. Let us strive to be among the blessed, among those who are not afraid to let their lives be formed and shaped by the God who is truth. No matter how dark it gets, the light shines in the darkness, and the darkness has not overcome it. "It is not darkness that dominates but the blinding brightness of [the light of Christ]. Death gives way to life, a life that dies no more. This is the truth that we should not only proclaim with our words, but above all with the witness of our lives."[175]

In this busy world that numbs us into complacency, it is good for us to be shocked by what we see — to stand still and take a long, hard look at what the culture is truly saying to us. But we can look upon this death and then choose to live with Christ in the heart of God and to savor the sweetness of the great and everlasting gift of the Father's never-ending love. Starting in the church of the home let us be beacons of hope in a world mired in the darkness of despair.

[174] Natalie Hudson, excerpt from a debate with Joyce Arthur on the issue of "Genetic Terminations" in the Center for Life Principles' *Life Compass* (March–April 2003): 4.

[175] Pope John Paul II, *Easter Vigil Homily*, April 14, 2001.

Chapter 6

Freedom in God's Mercy

Authentic Freedom in Christ

The period between the mid-1800s and the early 1960s saw the
rise of the black liberation movement from which emerged black
liberation theology.

> Beginning with the "black power" movement in 1966, black
> clergy in many denominations began to reassess the rela-
> tionship of the Christian church to the black community.
> Black clergy and theologians began to recognize the need for
> a completely new "starting point" in theology and insisted
> that this starting point be defined by people at the bottom
> and not the top of the socioeconomic ladder. Black theo-
> logians began to re-read the bible through the eyes of their
> slave grandparents and started to speak of God's solidarity
> with the oppressed of the earth.[176]

Liberation theology does not ask what the Church is, but rather
what it means to be the Church within the context of liberating
the poor and the oppressed. Thus, on this account, the Church's

---

[176] Ron Rhodes, "Black Theology, Black Power, and the Black Experience," Reasoning from the Scriptures Ministries, http://home.
earthlink.net/~ronrhodes/BlackTheology.html.

principal mission is to challenge injustice and identify Herself with the poor. According to this worldview, *the Church* is, properly speaking, the oppressed who have joined together seeking political means to remedy their subjugation, while, in contrast, the *Church's Magisterium and hierarchy* are members of the oppressor class, since it does not participate in the class struggle. As one synopsis put it:

> The people demand more than hierarchy, more than structure, more than rules and regulations from the Catholic Church. African Americans especially have needs that go beyond the racist institutional structures of the United States Catholic Church. African American Catholics carry within us … the rage of being despised and used by other human persons who deemed themselves superior to us. Our history unites us to Jesus, the Suffering Servant who dies alone and abandoned by his friends. We, too, have felt abandoned and alone in an alien country, and we still experience that abandonment and loneliness in the racist institutions of our society, perhaps particularly in the Church. It is a Church … that prefers the safety of hierarchy to the radical, countercultural mission of Jesus to challenge the status quo and minister to the people; the people of God with all their beautiful diversity and individual needs, the little people who are the Church. It is our responsibility to begin rewriting the history of the Church so that as a community we glorify God … not in materialistic, capitalistic expressions, but rather with a commitment to love, respect, forgive, and serve one another.[177]

This view of theology is shallow in its understanding of the hierarchical nature of the Church. It places the Magisterium on the

---

[177] Black Catholic Evangelization Forum, "Reclaiming and Rewriting Our Tradition," *Reach Out!* (November 1999): 1.

same level as a secular corporation, comparing Church hierarchy and authority to the obdurate structure of a worldwide conglomerate. This impoverished ecclesiology ignores and disparages the fact that the Church is both "already" (temporal and transcendent) and "not yet" (eschatological); She exists not merely as the Church on earth but also as the Church resplendent, as the glorified Body of Christ Jesus, Who established and sustains His Church as a *visible organization* through which He communicates grace and truth to all.[178] It is the *nature of the Church Herself*, founded and organized by Christ (Matt. 16:18; 18:18), that is holy, *in spite of* the people who are members of the Church, who are sinners in need of God's merciful love.

"The Church … is held, as a matter of faith, to be unfailingly holy. This is because Christ, the Son of God, who with the Father and the Spirit is hailed as 'alone holy,' loved the Church as his Bride, giving himself up for her so as to sanctify her; he joined her to himself as his body and endowed her with the gift of the Holy Spirit for the glory of God."[179] "United with Christ, the Church is sanctified by him; through him and with him she becomes sanctifying. 'All the activities of the Church are directed, as toward their end, to the sanctification of men in Christ and the glorification of God.' It is in the Church that 'the fullness of the means of salvation' has been deposited. It is in her that 'by the grace of God we acquire holiness.' "[180]

Thus, the Catholic Church, as the expert in humanity, "has the duty of proclaiming liberation in its deeper, fuller sense, the

[178] See Matthew 16:16–18; 18:18; Vatican Council II, *Lumen Gentium* 1–17.
[179] *Lumen Gentium* 39. Cf. Eph. 5:25–26, quoted in CCC 820.
[180] CCC 824, quoting *Sacrosanctum Concilium* 10; *Unitatis Redintegratio* 3; *Lumen Gentium* 48.

sense proclaimed and realized by Jesus Christ. That fuller liberation is liberation from everything that oppresses human beings,
but especially liberation from sin and the evil one."[181] To set us
free from the bondage of sin and death, we need the indwelling
love of Christ, which comes through the Holy Spirit, who leads us
into all truth. It is the truth that sets us free (see John 8:31–38).
And the truth of God's ever abundant and merciful love is rooted
in freedom, a freedom *from* and a freedom *for*—the freedom *from*
sin so that we can be free *for* God.

St. John Paul II called on Catholics to "help us all remember
that *authentic freedom* comes from accepting the truth and from
living one's life in accordance with it—and the full truth is found
only in Christ Jesus." He challenged: "Inspire us by your desire to
forgive—as Jesus forgave—and by your *desire to be reconciled* with
all the people of this nation, even those who would unjustly deny
you the full exercise of your human rights."[182]

Liberation theology fails to appreciate the reality of *personal*
sin, supplanting it with *social* sin—which is a true and important
concept, but not to the exclusion of personal sin. Thus, it conflates
the magisterial Church founded by Christ with the individuals
the Church comprises. Further, it fails to acknowledge that *choice*
is essential to spiritual freedom (Gen. 2:16), but this freedom is
diminished (though never completely annihilated) in the person
enslaved and corrupted by sin.

" 'The Church on earth is endowed already with a sanctity
that is real though imperfect.' In her members perfect holiness is
something yet to be acquired: 'Strengthened by so many and such

---

[181] Pope John Paul II, Opening Address, 1982 CELAM Conference,
Puebla, *Quade* (1982): 66–67.

[182] Pope John Paul II, Meeting with the black Catholics of New
Orleans, no. 3, my emphasis.

great means of salvation, all the faithful, whatever their condition or state—though each in his own way—are called by the Lord to that perfection of sanctity by which the Father himself is perfect.'"[183] "But while in the most Blessed Virgin the Church has already reached that perfection whereby she exists without spot or wrinkle, the faithful still strive to conquer sin and increase in holiness."[184]

When we use our freedom to conform ourselves to God's holy will—to be the person He created us to be by living in a way commensurate with this truth—then we are spiritually free. We realize spiritual freedom when we lovingly accept God's grace in accord with who we are called to be.[185] When we are spiritually free, we are liberated from our fallen condition and directed toward union with God. At the center of God's plan for human freedom is the fact that He created man in light of Christ so that we can participate in God's own Trinitarian life. This is humanity's truest identity.

At first glance, living according to God's truth seems burdensome. After all, following commandments and living according to a moral code goes against society's understanding of freedom. In God's design for authentic freedom, though, laws and commandments are at the service of the practice of love. Remember: The commandments are summed up in the two Great Commandments: Love the Lord your God with your whole heart, soul, mind and with all your strength, and love your neighbor as yourself (Luke 10:27). It's true that mindless obedience to the commandments is an imperfect freedom, even a partial slavery—until it becomes our

---

[183] CCC 825, quoting *Lumen Gentium* 48, 11.

[184] *Lumen Gentium* 65, quoted in in CCC 829.

[185] See Pope John Paul II, *Veritatis Splendor* 84–87, especially no. 85: *"The Crucified Christ reveals the authentic meaning of freedom; he lives it fully in the total gift of himself* and calls his disciples to share in his freedom."

delight to obey them. The truth is that "the more one does what is good, the freer one becomes. There is no true freedom except in the service of what is good and just. The choice to disobey and do evil is an abuse of freedom and leads to 'the slavery of sin.'"[186]

Humanity is created yearning for fullness while still mired in concupiscence. Due to our fallen nature, we become frustrated when we come to the realization that we are finite and incomplete, that we cannot on our own love as God loves. Spiritual freedom comes when we love with the love of Christ, but sin impedes our efforts to make this choice. It is in this way that sin is enslaving: It binds us to disordered love. The more sin becomes a habit, the more it binds us to the fleeting goods of this world—our disordered attachments. Sin establishes an addictive pattern and keeps us from conforming to the truth of our being.

Our free choice needs to be set free, and it is Christ who accomplishes this through his Death and Resurrection. We need God's love dwelling within us to free us from the bondage of sin so we can become witnesses of that love to the world.

The Church for All People

Our Lord says, "Everyone who exalts himself will be humbled, but the one who humbles himself will be exalted" (see Matt. 23:12; Luke 14:11). Humility does not mean having low self-esteem or being overly pious, because true humility is not about you. It is not thinking less of yourself; it is thinking of yourself less.

What does humility look like? When Solomon became king of Israel, he asked God to give him "'an understanding mind to govern your people, that I may discern between good and evil.' ... It pleased the Lord that Solomon had asked this. And God said to

---

[186] CCC 1733; John 8:31-38.

him, 'Because you have asked this, and have not asked for yourself long life or riches or the life of your enemies, but have asked for yourself understanding to discern what is right, behold, I now do according to your word'" (1 Kings 3:9-12).

Fr. Tolton was the model of humility. A Vatican official from the Collegium Urbanum de Propaganda Fide in Rome, where Fr. Tolton studied for the priesthood, noted that "Augustine Tolton is highly commended for self-sacrifice, piety, and other virtues. He is very capable and especially trained for the discharge of the sacred ministry."[187] The life of Fr. Tolton teaches us that being humble means living with the realization that we are constantly in the presence of God—that everything we think, say, and do is done before the Lord; that everything we are, everyone we meet, and all that we experience in this world are His creation; that every time we sin—every time we choose against the will of Christ and the teachings of His Church—we separate ourselves from being able to have a personal encounter with God.

Yet, in our weakness, we often spurn humility and turn our backs on God, believing that we know better than He does: when we think we are the author of our own success; when we live by our own rules apart from the Church; when we ignore God's plan. In our pride, we too often live ignorant of the awareness that we are forever in the presence of God.

True humility can begin only when our eyes are fixed upon Our Lord Jesus Christ. Peter knelt before Jesus and said, "Depart from me, for I am a sinful man" (Luke 5:8). Mary Magdalene wept at the feet of Jesus and dried her tears with her hair (Luke 7:36–50). The Roman centurion told Jesus that he was not worthy that Jesus should enter under his roof (Matt. 8:8). The humble recognition of our own sinfulness allows us to experience the mercy of God.

---

[187] Hemesath, *Slave to Priest*, 176.

Fr. Augustus Tolton

When Jesus speaks to the Apostles concerning the grace of true humility, He uses a parable rebuking those who assume places of honor (Luke 14:7–11). In the end, Jesus Himself models this behavior for His Apostles by becoming the servant of all.

The Lord Jesus preached the truth—and was killed for it. Many saints of the Church, such as Agnes, Lucy, and Perpetua, were tortured and killed because they would not compromise their most beloved and prized possession—the great gift of their Catholic Faith. Yet today, almost daily, we hear of so-called Catholic politicians and colleges that undermine and ignore their Catholic identity for worldly recognition and thirty pieces of silver. The question we must ask ourselves is this: If it were a crime today to be a follower of Jesus, would there be enough evidence to convict us?

When we are faced with the Cross in our lives, what choice will we make? Will we be the bad thief, who used his free will to choose against God—the easy way out—and who mocked and ridiculed Our Lord in the process? Or will we be the good thief, the repentant sinner, who freely chose the path that leads to the infinite, life-giving love of the Father—and to whom Jesus promised: "Today you will be with me in Paradise" (Luke 23:43)?

> When life is hard and apparently hopeless, we can be confident that this darkness of ours can be taken up into the great darkness of redemption through which the light of Easter dawns. And when what is required of us seems too burdensome, when the pains become unbearable and the fate we are asked to accept seems simply meaningless—then we have come very close to the man nailed on the Cross at the Place of the Skull, for he has already undergone this on our behalf and in unimaginable intensity. When surrounded by apparent meaninglessness, all we can do is wait and endure like the Crucified facing the dark abyss of death. Beyond

this abyss there waits for us something that we cannot see … namely, a light in which all the world's pain is treasured and cherished in the ever-open heart of God.[188]

Then we shall be allowed, like the apostle Thomas, to put our hand into His gaping wound and realize, in a very real way, that God's love transcends all human understanding.[189] We will come to know and experience, as the life of Fr. Augustus Tolton so eloquently expressed, that the Cross is the meaning of sacrifice—and that the Cross is the meaning of love.

Fr. Tolton never wavered from the Church, despite enduring the cross of a lifetime of racial animosity. In the face of such intense bigotry and hatred, why did he remain in the Catholic Church? As we reflect on the life of this noble priest, the reason becomes clear: Fr. Tolton was able to discern what many Catholics who leave the Church today fail to perceive and do not fully appreciate: that what the Catholic Church *teaches* is true, good, and beautiful despite the hypocrisy and contradiction of Church members who do not *live* the faith they profess. Fr. Tolton always acknowledged the great gift of his Catholic Faith, and recognized that sin and weakness are not greater or more powerful than the strength of objective truth found in Catholicism. Fr. Tolton was a visionary who saw far beyond issues of race and politics, looking inward—into the heart of the Church Herself.

The Catholic Church deplores a double slavery—that of the mind and that of the body. She endeavors to free us of both. I was a poor slave boy, but the priests of the Church did

---

[188] Hans Urs von Balthasar, *You Crown the Year with Your Goodness: Sermons Through the Liturgical Year* (San Francisco: Ignatius Press, 1989), 86.

[189] Ibid.

not disdain me. It was through the influence of one of them that I became what I am.... It was the priests of the Church who taught me to pray and to forgive my persecutors.... It was through the direction of a School Sister of Notre Dame ... that I ... beheld for the first time the glimmering light of truth and the majesty of the Church.... The Church which knows and makes no distinction in race and color [calls us] all. When the Church does all of this, is she not a true liberator of the race? In this Church we do not have to fight for our rights because we are black.... The Church is broad and liberal [i.e., generous]. She is the Church for our people.[190]

This perspective is echoed beautifully in the words of St. John Paul the Great, who addressed black Catholics in the United States with these words:

It is important to realize that there is no black Church, no white Church, no American Church; but there is and must be, in the one Church of Jesus Christ, a home for blacks, whites, Americans, every culture and race. "The Church is catholic ... because she is able to present in every human context the revealed truth, preserved by her intact in its divine content, in such a way as to bring it into contact with the lofty thoughts and just expectations of every individual and every people."[191]

Let us pray that, as the universal Church strives to overcome the slavery of personal sin, She may, living in the heart of Christ, better recognize and more fully appreciate the abundant gifts and talents that every member contributes to the Church. May we come to a

---

[190] Hemesath, *Slave to Priest*, 185.
[191] Pope John Paul II, Meeting with the black Catholics of New Orleans, no. 7; cf. *Slavorum Apostoli*, no. 18.

deeper understanding that the distinct charisms and rich cultural heritage of Catholics throughout the world are rooted in a covenant relationship with God—a relationship that transcends all races and colors. It is Christ who binds us all together and makes us one in Him. As such, a true theology of multicultural diversity—grounded in the unique traditions and expressions of a people—should not separate itself from the authority of the Church but, instead, should integrate magisterial teaching into its methodology and practice. When the Church shares the one heartbeat of apostolic faith, the invaluable contributions of Catholics of color throughout history, like Fr. Augustus Tolton, will serve as both the foundation and point of departure for uniting the one Body of Christ, making Christ's kingdom a more present and meaningful reality in our world.

Freedom and Divine Mercy

Divine mercy is the Father's merciful love, which overcomes evil and suffering in the world. Divine mercy becomes visible in and through the person of Jesus Christ—through His words, His actions, His Death on the Cross, and His Resurrection. Through Jesus Christ, God the Father also becomes visible in His mercy (John 14:9–10). Those who seek and find mercy in Jesus experience true freedom in God's divine mercy and love.

How does Jesus reveal the Father's merciful love?

Jesus is the Incarnation. The Incarnation is the fullest expression of God's mercy: God became man in order to redeem us from sin, suffering, and evil. Mercy, in the person of Jesus, is love's response to suffering.

Jesus reveals mercy to us in His teaching. The Lord's parables and sermons all communicate mercy in human terms that can be understood and put into practice by all humanity.

Jesus is the model and source of mercy by His actions. Jesus' actions include His ministry, His Passion, and His Death. His actions also include miracles: extraordinary signs of mercy, love, and compassion that showed the presence of the Kingdom of God.

How does the Church, founded by Christ, reveal the Father's merciful love?

The Church professes and proclaims mercy by contemplating and living the message of Christ found in Scripture and Tradition, particularly through Her participation in the Eucharist and in the sacrament of Reconciliation, resulting in continual forgiveness and conversion.

The Church practices mercy through evangelization, by imploring mercy for others and, in turn, receiving mercy from others. In giving and receiving mercy, the spirit of equality, justice, and forgiveness is forged in the hearts of the faithful.

The Church depends on mercy for Herself and seeks it through prayer, petitions, and works of charity, which are offered to the Father and which implore mercy according to the needs of man in the modern world.

Divine mercy, then, is the source of human freedom and healing from sin. "The longing for [healing] will be complete and effective only to the extent that they reach — in order to heal it — that original wound which is the root of all other wounds: namely sin.... [Healing], therefore (in order to be complete), necessarily requires liberation from sin, which is to be rejected in its deepest roots."[192]

---

[192] John Paul II, Post-synodal Apostolic Exhortation *Reconciliatio et Paenitentia* (Reconciliation and Penance) (December 2, 1984), nos. 3 and 4.

It is probably true that most of us have been hurt in some way by someone we love. All too often we remain oppressed by the resulting negative emotions. We bring the baggage of anxiety, rejection, anger, fear, and a distorted self-image into our relationships, and then often we cannot fully explain the reasons why those relationships are not joyful and fulfilling.

What does this "baggage" look like?

Maybe you have an abusive ex-husband who beat you while he was drunk.

Maybe your spouse was unfaithful and, even though you may have "reconciled," the infidelity has made you insecure not only about your future, but also about your decision to marry in the first place.

Maybe a friend got you hooked on alcohol, drugs, or pornography.

Maybe you were raped in college. Maybe you were the rapist, taking advantage of a vulnerable young woman instead of protecting and safeguarding her dignity.

Maybe you were abused by a family member or a trusted friend.

Maybe, like Fr. Tolton, you were bullied in school because you were of a different race, wore glasses, had an accent, or were poor. Maybe you were the bully, taking out your anger and frustration on others weaker than you.

Maybe you had an abortion, or maybe you participated in or encouraged someone to end the life of her unborn child.

Maybe you are alienated from your children or grandchildren who are no longer practicing their Faith. Or maybe you are estranged from your parents, who disowned you when you became Catholic.

Maybe you are angry all the time.

Maybe you suffer from depression or oppressive anxiety.

Yet Jesus' invitation to us all is peace. *Peace I leave with you; my peace I give to you; not as the world gives do I give to you"* (John

14:27). How can we acquire His peace for our wounded memories and broken relationships? With the life of Fr. Augustus Tolton as the source for moving forward in faith, I offer four suggestions that I have used in my own healing. They are not easy, but they are ways we can respond to Christ's call to pick up our cross and follow Him.

1. *Do not bury the hurts of the past.* It may be painful, but it is important to remember and feel the emotions that emerged after what happened to you or what you did to someone else. Burying past pain and hurt will not facilitate healing; we must acknowledge that what occurred "back then" did take place. Feel the anger, the resentment, the bitterness, the emptiness. When we bring these memories of the past before the Lord, especially through the heart of His Blessed Mother in Eucharistic Adoration, then we will find the healing and peace that our hearts yearn for and desire (Luke 2:35). "Let me hear what God the Lord will speak, for he will speak peace to his people, to his saints, to those who turn to him in their hearts." (Psalm 85:8).

2. *Realize that you can defeat the Goliaths in your life only with the weapons of God.* David heard that the Philistine warrior Goliath had issued a challenge to the soldiers of Israel. Goliath had mocked and defied the Israelite army for forty consecutive days, but Saul's men were afraid to confront such a formidable opponent. It is easy to see why: Goliath was an extraordinarily intimidating figure, standing approximately nine feet, nine inches high. He wore 125 pounds of armor and had a spear that weighed just over 15 pounds. In the presence of Goliath, the Israelites "were dismayed and greatly afraid" (1 Sam. 17:11).

Goliath represents the hurts of our past. Many of us are so intimidated by the size, scope, and depth of this onslaught that we are paralyzed by fear; we say and do nothing. What is the "Goliath" in your life that is preventing you from being the person God has called you to be? What is it that has you so scared that you are more comfortable living as a slave to the past rather than living free as a son or daughter of God? "For you did not receive the spirit of slavery to fall back into fear, but you have received the spirit of sonship" (Rom. 8:15).

The Goliaths in our lives cause us to fear, and thereby they empty us of God's love. The flow of grace through daily prayer and the sacraments, however, fills us up again with His love so that we can truly become whole and complete in the eyes of God. "There is no fear in love, but perfect love casts out fear" (1 John 4:18). Filled with confidence in God's love, we can now face Goliath with confidence: "The Lord is my light and my help; whom shall I fear? The Lord is the stronghold of my life; before whom shall I shrink?" (Ps. 27:1).

> Saul clothed David with his armor; he put a helmet of bronze on his head, and clothed him with a coat of mail. And David belted on his sword over his armor, and he tried in vain to go, for he was not used to them. Then David said to Saul, "I cannot go with these; for I am not used to them." And David put them off. (1 Sam. 17:38–39)

David tried to put on armor so he could look like Goliath, but he was unsuccessful. He realized that, for this battle, he needed to put on the armor of God and fight with the weapons of faith.

David "took his staff in his hand, and chose five smooth stones from the brook, and put them in his shepherd's bag or wallet; his sling was in his hand, and he drew near to the Philistine" (1 Sam. 17:40). In the spiritual sense of this passage, the sling and stones are reminiscent of the Rosary, each stone representing a decade of Hail Marys and reflecting one of the mysteries of our salvation. They also represent the five wounds of Christ, Our Lord's battle scars in His victory over sin and death. In our battle against the Goliath within us, the Rosary is most certainly the weapon of choice. But we also have Eucharistic Adoration, the Chaplet of Divine Mercy, the Memorare, Lectio Divina, the Stations of the Cross, the Liturgy of the Hours, and innumerable novenas, just to name a few.

David then confronted Goliath. Unwavering in his faith and armed with a simple weapon, David embarked on what his kinsmen would surely have considered a suicide mission. After Goliath mocked David and threatened his life, David said:

> You come to me with a sword and with a spear and with a javelin; but I come to you in the name of the LORD of hosts, the God of the armies of Israel, whom you have defied. This day the LORD will deliver you into my hand, and I will strike you down, and cut off your head; and I will give the dead bodies of the host of the Philistines this day to the birds of the air and to the wild beasts of the earth; that all the earth may know that there is a God in Israel, and that all this assembly may know that the LORD saves not with sword and spear; for the battle is the LORD's and he will give you into our hand. (1 Sam. 17:45–47)

We may have convinced ourselves that the painful memories that have controlled and enslaved us for so long are too powerful. When we think like that, Satan wins. We must remember that we are not alone in this fight: The battle belongs to the Lord, and He has already won the war through His victory over death on the Cross. By the witness of our lives and as living images of the crucified Christ, we must send a clear and strong message to the Goliath within us that there is a God who saves, and His name is Jesus Christ!

3. *Make a general confession.* A general confession is confessing to a priest all the sins you have committed in your lifetime. You may have already confessed these sins and had them forgiven, but general confession is not only about forgiveness; it is about healing.

It is true that Christ has already forgiven us and "forgotten" about our past sins (see Ezek. 18:21–22: "If a wicked man turns away from all his sins which he has committed ... he shall surely live; he shall not die. None of the transgressions which he has committed shall be remembered against him"), but we often have a difficult time forgiving ourselves. There is something cathartic about revisiting the past and seeing how much progress we have made on our spiritual journey — and how far we still need to go. A general confession helps us to realize that while the past shapes us into the person we are today, the past does not determine our future.

4. *Ask forgiveness from the person who hurt you.* This may be the most difficult step of all. You may be asking yourself, "Why should I ask for forgiveness when I did nothing wrong?" That may be true, but it is also not the point. Christ calls us to be conduits of mercy to others. In the beautiful Divine Mercy image, the blood and water that gushed forth from the pierced heart of Jesus are depicted as rays of love and mercy flowing *from* the heart of Jesus and into the world. When we extend mercy, not only does the other person receive mercy *from* us, but they also, in a sense, give mercy *to* us, since we experience the mercy of Christ in being allowed to show mercy to others. When we overcome the burdens of the past by extending mercy to others, we experience mercy ourselves.

Once again, Fr. Tolton serves as a model for us. Despite the fact that he was mercilessly persecuted by a fellow clergyman in Quincy, America's first black priest was not deterred "from making repeated efforts toward reaching an understanding [and] made use of every opportunity to the gain the friendship and good will of the white priest."[193]

These four suggestions for finding healing in God's mercy are difficult but not insurmountable, since nothing is impossible with

---

[193] Hemesath, *Slave to Priest*, 186.

God (Matt. 19:26). Consider this analogy: When you walk into your kitchen, you notice that your preschool child is holding a very large, sharp knife by the blade. Would you proceed to grab the knife out of the child's hand? Of course not. Instead, you would say something like this: "Hi, honey. What have you got there? Let me see. Oh wow, look at that! Can you show it to me, sweetie? Can you open your hand and give it to me?" As the child slowly releases the blade and lifts it toward you, you would then gently remove the knife. Children do this because they love and trust their parents and want to share what they have with them.

God the Father wants to do the same thing for us, His children. God sees the knife of hostility, trepidation, and past sufferings that haunt us. Through His divine mercy, God wants to remove the pain of those memories from our hearts. In the four steps outlined above, God says to us, "My child, whom I love with my whole being, what have you got there? Let me see. Oh wow, look at that! That's the knife of abuse and neglect that you've suffered over the years; the knife of anxiety and fear that you've held inside for as long as you can remember; the knife of the embarrassing, shameful acts of your past. Can you show it to me? Can you open your hand and give it to me?" Just as we do not want our children to hold on to something that is dangerous and can hurt them, so God our loving Father does not want us to hold on to the hurts of the past. As we slowly open our hand and lift the knife toward our Father, He will gently remove it from our possession. We let Him do this because we love and trust God and want to share everything we have and everything we are with Him. This is how we, the precious children of our heavenly Father, participate in the divine nature (2 Pet. 1:4)—through loving and life-giving communion with Jesus our Lord, in the unity of the Holy Spirit.

Unconditional forgiveness and showing mercy are decisions, definitive acts of the will—not just feelings. We must ask Jesus for healing of our deep-seated brokenness, and then pray to the Holy Spirit that the burdened hearts of our past lives may be washed clean and made pure by the Most Precious Blood of Jesus. "O purify me, then I shall be clean; O wash me, I shall be whiter than snow" (Ps. 51:9).

Mercy is going above and beyond justice out of love for another person. Mercy responds to evil and human suffering out of love. "O my Strength, it is you to whom I turn, for you, O God, are my stronghold, the God who shows me love" (Ps. 59:18).

A Biblical Parallel: Trusting in God's Divine Mercy

Quite often, after I lead a parish mission, someone approaches who wants to spend time talking about a serious issue in their life. This past Lent, I spoke with several teenage girls in different parts of the country who had very similar stories. One of them, a sixteen-year-old, was abused as a child and, as a result, had been very sexually active, had abused drugs and alcohol, and was dating a twenty-three-year-old man. But this was not the person that her family and friends saw. They saw a dynamic, vibrant member of the parish youth group who was respected and admired by her peers, and who gave testimonial talks about her relationship with God.

We talked for over an hour and a half. She cried most of the time as she opened her heart to me, sharing some deeply personal parts of her life. She was clearly anxious and in tremendous pain. She knew that she was acting contrary to God's will and had to make a major change in her life, a change that would include the very painful decision to end a relationship with the man she had grown to love, but who had actively pursued an illicit and illegal relationship with her. She was scared and could not let go because she was afraid to trust God.

Fr. Augustus Tolton

After encouraging her to seek God's mercy and peace in the sacrament of Reconciliation, I said this to her: "Right now, there is a young man on his knees praying to meet someone like you. This is a young man who is willing to give his heart, his mind, his soul, his body to you and to only you, and to the children you will have together, for the rest of your life until your death. That is a love worth waiting for because that is a love worth dying for."

A love worth dying for. This is the depth of the love and mercy that God the Father has for us: His Son endured the Cross, carrying the weight of our sins on his shoulders. In His tremendous suffering, Jesus was allowed to experience — in His human nature — what it is like for us when we are going through something really difficult and feel that God is not there for us (Ps. 22:2–3). He eventually even endured death, the ultimate consequence of sin. But by His Resurrection, Christ has conquered sin; He has triumphed over death and has shattered the gates of Hell. God's love is so immense, and its power so limitless, and its embrace so tender and intimate, that Love Himself brings forth life.

When Jesus appeared to St. Margaret Mary Alacoque, He showed her His heart to demonstrate how much He loves us.[194] He said to her, "Behold the Heart which has so loved men that it has spared nothing, even to exhausting and consuming Itself, in order to testify Its love; and in return, I receive from the greater part only ingratitude, by their irreverence and sacrilege."[195] He is loved so little in return because we do not truly believe in the love, the promise, and the mercy of God the Father.

---

[194] The next several paragraphs are inspired by a Divine Mercy homily given by Fr. Robert Altier posted on Free Republic, http://www.freerepublic.com/focus/f-religion/1615266/posts.

[195] See *The Autobiography of St. Margaret Mary*, repr. ed. (Charlotte, NC: TAN Books, 2012), 95.

Our Lord told St. Faustina of the mercy He wants to give to the world, if only we will believe in His love. If we are honest with ourselves, we will realize that we are often lukewarm at best. Sunday after Sunday we hear the Word of God and receive Our Lord in the Most Blessed Sacrament of the Eucharist—and yet we walk away, for the most part, unchanged even while knowing full well that Christ is calling us to change our lives and to become one with Him. We allow ourselves just enough faith to be comfortable until that faith calls us to stand up for the truth that makes us uncomfortable. Then, like the apostles, we lock the doors of our minds and hearts, cowering in the fear of being rejected and unpopular.

Each one of us, when we were consecrated to the Most Holy Trinity on the day of our Baptism, was set aside for a holy purpose. To do God's work, we cannot think or act like everyone else; rather, we are to follow in the footsteps of Our Lord and Savior Jesus Christ.

Jesus appeared to His apostles and said, "Peace be with you" (John 20:21), precisely because they were not at peace: They were afraid. Today, because we do not trust in God's mercy, we keep Jesus at arm's length so that our lives do not have to change. We do not want to let Jesus get too close because we know that when we do, His tender mercy will transform us.

It is at these times that we must take comfort in the Father's endless mercy and be at peace with being vulnerable before the Lord. Jesus breathed on the apostles, and they were given the authority to forgive sins—our sins. When we really know that our sins are forgiven, we have nothing to fear. If we truly believe in the promises of Our Lord, we can be at peace. We live in a time when the mercy of God is more necessary than ever before, but as Our Lord told St. Paul, "Where sin abounds, grace abounds all the more" (see Rom. 5:20). Because there is so much sin in the world, the Lord provides an overwhelming abundance of grace that is available to us in the sacraments.

In that famous and beautiful image of Divine Mercy, the Lord comes to us and points to His heart, where two rays of love pour out into the world. One ray is white, depicting the waters of Baptism; the other is red, representing the blood of Jesus Christ present in the Blessed Sacrament of the Eucharist.

Sacraments are not empty rituals. The Mass is not designed for us simply to go through the motions and walk out unchanged. What happens in all the sacraments, especially at Mass and in the sacrament of Reconciliation, are realities more profound and powerful than anything we can ever hope to experience in this world. The worst sin we could ever commit is like a drop of water in the ocean of God's infinite mercy. His love for us is endless, beyond anything we could ever grasp or imagine. As big as our sins might be, they are nothing for the Lord.

When we come before the priest in Confession and hear those beautiful words of absolution, we walk out with the unshakable knowledge that our sins have been removed from our souls. In His mercy, the Lord looks us right in the face, as He looked at Thomas two thousand years ago, and He says, "Doubt no longer, but believe" (see John 20:27).

When we give ourselves over to God's divine mercy in the sacraments—and when we love with a love worth dying for and are no longer afraid and in doubt—we will have the courage to place our hands in the wounds of Christ and profess with confidence and joy and faithfulness, "My Lord and my God" (John 20:28).

Heavenly Father, for the sake of Your Son's sorrowful Passion, have mercy on us and on the whole world.

I end my reflections here by offering a prayer I composed in Eucharistic Adoration that was inspired by the life and legacy of

Fr. Augustus John Tolton, a faithful disciple of Christ in the order of the Blessed Virgin Mary:

> God our Father, through the prayers of your handmaid Mary, may we be obedient in faith so that we can be free to love You with our whole being. As Your Word filled Mary's womb, may the precious Body and Blood of Your Son fill us with the Holy Spirit and unite us with You in an intimate, personal, and life-giving bond of love here on earth until we are united with You forever in Heaven.
>
> Almighty Father, in Your divine providence, You gave the people You created and love the gift of salvation in and through Your Son Jesus Christ, born of the Virgin Mary. Just as Mary said yes to Your holy will, may we say yes to You by using the grace You have given us to transform the world from the inside out. Just as Mary bore Your Son in her womb, may we who receive the same Jesus in the Eucharist gain the strength to stay true to our Catholic Faith in a world that makes it difficult for us to accept the truth. Just as Mary gave birth to Your Word, may we too give birth to Jesus in our own lives, using the unique and special gifts given to each one of us to evangelize; to be faithful witnesses of Your love and life within this culture of sin and death.
>
> Merciful Father, Mary's immaculate purity enabled her to enter into the sufferings of Christ in the obedience of faith and in compassionate love. May we bear the trials of this life with Mary's heart, so that in our weakness Your glory will shine forth through us, that we may be fully and completely the people You created us to be, made in Your image and likeness. We ask this through Our Lord Jesus Christ, Your Son, who lives and reigns with You in the unity of the Holy Spirit, one God forever and ever. Amen.

Toward Sainthood

We are all called to be saints (1 Cor. 1:2). The primary purpose of canonization in the Catholic Church is officially to declare that a particular person, whose life of heroic virtue serves as a model for us all, is actually in Heaven. We honor (*not* worship) saints and ask for their intercession before the Lord Jesus. The investigation process that leads to canonization seeks to ensure that God truly is working through the person, demonstrating that he or she is now with Him for all eternity.

Being canonized means, among other things, that the canonized person's name is added to the official record of saints and that the faithful can invoke the saint's name in public prayers. In addition, churches may be named after the saint and Mass can be offered in his or her honor.

Interest in the life of Fr. Augustus Tolton has grown rapidly over the last few decades, due in large part to the efforts of the Most Reverend Joseph N. Perry, auxiliary bishop of Chicago, and the 2006 Ignatius Press rerelease of Sister Caroline Hemesath's landmark biography, *From Slave to Priest: The Inspirational Story of Fr. Augustine Tolton (1854–1897)*.

Fr. Augustus Tolton

On February 24, 2011, Francis Cardinal George, then the archbishop of Chicago, officially opened the cause for the canonization of Fr. Tolton with the following pronouncement.

Edict
Cause of the Beatification and Canonization of
Fr. August Tolton

In accordance with article 43 of the 2007 Instruction of the Congregation for Causes of Saints, *Sanctorum Mater*, I, the undersigned Ordinary of the Archdiocese of Chicago, declare that I have received and accepted the petition for the Cause of beatification and canonization of the Servant of God, Fr. Augustus Tolton [1854–1897].

Therefore, the Cause having been officially opened during the formal hearing held at St. James Chapel at the Archdiocesan Pastoral Center, on this the 24th day of February, 2011, I am directing the assigned personnel of the ecclesiastical tribunal to carry out all necessary steps to instruct the diocesan phase of the Cause, inclusive of hearing witnesses regarding Tolton's virtues and reputation of holiness. In addition, I encourage all those who can give testimony, even should they have negative proof, to come forward and contact the aforementioned tribunal. Moreover, those who possess writings of any kind or any other information regarding Fr. Tolton are urged to put that at the tribunal's disposition.

All things henceforth serving the honor of God,

Given at Chicago, Illinois
the 24th day of February 2011
Francis Cardinal George, OMI
Archbishop of Chicago

Less than a year later, on February 13, 2012, the Sacred Congregation for Causes of Saints at the Vatican granted the title "Servant of God" to Fr. Augustus Tolton and ordered that the Archdiocese of Chicago proceed with the diocesan inquiry into his life and virtues.

The Archdiocese of Chicago completed the diocesan phase of the investigation in mid-2014. Documents supporting the cause for sainthood for Fr. Tolton were sent to the Congregation for Causes of Saints. The next year, the congregation declared the juridical validity of the archdiocesan inquiry, thereby clearing the way for Fr. Tolton's cause to proceed.

On December 9–10, 2016, Fr. Tolton's remains were exhumed from St. Peter Cemetery in Quincy, Illinois. A medical examiner, as well as forensic and anthropologist specialists, investigated for signs of miraculous incorruption of the priest's body. The report of the exhumation was sent to Rome, and relics from the body were collected for veneration, should the cause proceed all the way to canonization.

On March 8, 2018, historical consultants for the Congregation for the Causes of Saints reviewed the official documents on the Servant of God Fr. Augustus Tolton and voted overwhelmingly that the cause could move forward—eventually to the desk of the Holy Father.

Following this announcement, Bishop Perry, the diocesan postulator for Fr. Tolton's cause, called the approval a "very positive sign" and noted its significance for the African American Catholic community: "Fr. Tolton ... was a pioneer of his era for inclusiveness, drawing both blacks and whites to his parish in Quincy. However, due to his race, he suffered discrimination and condemnation. The beatification and canonization of Fr. Tolton will signal a significant milestone in the history of black Catholicism in the United States."[196]

---

[196] CNA/EWTN News, "American Runaway Slave-Turned-Priest Moves Closer to Beatification," *National Catholic Register*, May

Fr. Augustus Tolton

The *National Catholic Register* notes that "the next step in his cause for canonization will be in February 2019, when a theological commission with the Congregation for the Causes of Saints will further investigate his life and virtue and consider granting him the title of 'Venerable,' which must receive papal approval. After that step, the cause would move forward toward beatification, for which a miracle through his intercession must be approved."[197]

Let us all pray the following canonization prayer, composed by Bishop Perry, with the intention that Servant of God Augustus John Tolton will one day be recognized as a saint by the Church he served so well.

O God, we give You thanks for Your servant and priest, Fr. Augustus Tolton, who labored among us in times of contradiction, times that were both beautiful and paradoxical. His ministry helped lay the foundation for a truly Catholic gathering in faith in our time. We stand in the shadow of his ministry. May his life continue to inspire us and imbue us with that confidence and hope that will forge a new evangelization for the Church we love.

Father in Heaven, Fr. Tolton's suffering service sheds light upon our sorrows; we see them through the prism of Your Son's Passion and Death. If it be your will, O God, glorify Your servant, Fr. Tolton, by granting the favor I now request through his intercession (*mention your request*) so that all may know the goodness of this priest whose memory looms large in the Church he loved.

14, 2018, http://www.ncregister.com/daily-news/american-run-away-slave-turned-priest-moves-closer-to-beatification. For the most up-to-date information about Fr. Tolton and his canonization cause, please visit the official Fr. Tolton website, http://www.toltoncanonization.org/.

[197] Ibid.

Toward Sainthood

Complete what You have begun in us that we might work for the fulfillment of Your kingdom. Not to us the glory, but glory to You, O God, through Jesus Christ, Your Son and our Lord; Father, Son, and Holy Spirit, You are our God, living and reigning forever and ever. Amen.

About the Author

Deacon Harold Burke-Sivers is an internationally renowned speaker, author, and preacher. He holds a Bachelor of Arts Degree in Economics and Business Administration from the University of Notre Dame, and a Master of Theological Studies Degree from the University of Dallas. He has appeared as a guest on numerous international Catholic radio programs and is the host or co-host of several popular series on the Eternal Word Television Network. Deacon Harold, a Benedictine Oblate, is the author of the best-selling book *Behold the Man: A Catholic Vision of Male Spirituality*, published by Ignatius Press, and co-author of the acclaimed new book *Ignite: Read the Bible Like Never Before*. He is a member of the Fellowship of Catholic Scholars and the Confraternity of Catholic Clergy. Most importantly, Deacon Harold is married to his lovely wife, Colleen, and they have four beautiful children.